Liverpool Football Club
An A-Z

Liverpool Football Club
An A-Z

Darren Phillips

Aureus

For my Nan

First Published 2003

Cover photograph : Souness holds the European Cup aloft after Liverpool's victory against AS Roma in 1984. ©ASP (www.sporting-heroes.net)
Back cover photograph ©Darren Phillips

Photographs on pages 15, 115 & 147 © Darren Phillips. All other photographs ©Sporting Heroes

ISBN 1 899750 26 6

Printed in Great Britain.

A catalogue record for this book is available from the British Library.

Aureus Publishing Limited
Castle Court
Castle-upon-Alun
St. Bride's Major
Vale of Glamorgan
CF32 0TN

Tel: (01656) 880033 Fax: (01656) 880033
Int. tel: +44 1656 880033 Int. fax: +44 1656 880033

E-mail: sales@aureus.co.uk
Web site: www.aureus.co.uk

About the author

Exiled from his native Merseyside the 32 year old author resides in the parochial splendour of Heywood, Lancashire – an essential relocation, as his obsession with The Reds is narrowly eclipsed by the love for his wife, Donna, and children Sophie and Sam.

This Kop season ticket holder and Anfield regular for over a decade has witnessed some of his club's greatest moments and personally knows many of the players mentioned in this book.

Among his other journalism and writing credits are freelance contributions to the now defunct Liverpool FC centred magazine - Xtra Time.

Darren Phillips started as a Non-league sports reporter for the Liverpool Daily Post and Echo, Football Echo, St Helens Star and St Helens Reporter. In the more recent past he has worked on projects connected with Preston North End, Burnley, Wigan Athletic and Bolton Wanderers.

His first book: 'Better Than the Brazillians' chronicles the club's record breaking 1987-88 season. They were unbeaten for 29 games from the start of a campaign, sweeping all challengers before them as they powered towards a title they would win by 9 clear points and blasting their way to Wembley in the FA Cup - conceding just one goal in the process.

Since that first book he has worked on another A-Z title concerning a team with contrasting fortunes to that of Liverpool. Rochdale FC have a rich if varied history and the book proved a huge success in the Lancashire town.

Author's Preface

Wistful nostalgia. That's what I'm told an exercise like this is and to be honest it's true. I have always gained a certain amount of satisfaction from leafing through reference books and learning more about the people that have made Liverpool Football Club the institution that it is. The achievements we have all shared have given me equal satisfaction.

It's an enthusiasm I've tried to reflect in this book and one which, hopefully, the reader will not only share but use to retain confidence in the club. We have endured difficult seasons to say the least but let's all remember what we are, have been and can be once more. After all we are Liverpool. Still the most successful club in British and European history with a record which is unparalleled and unique.

As for the content of the book every major event and some not so outstanding times over the club's history is included from the club's formation to the unique cup treble of the 2000-01 season and onwards. Disagreements over the choice of players included could be waged. I've no doubt somebody's favourite has been excluded while they may scratch their head while reading the career history of a player who they think barely merits a mention. The criteria for selecting individuals are not uniform. In general players with 100 appearances or more for The Reds in league and cup games have been included though other centurions have not. This is purely down to value judgements on my behalf and those whose opinions were canvassed.

Those players with less than 100 games to their credit you may read about were as a rule selected if their contribution to the club was viewed as worthy of a few words, or if they had been involved in a monumental or unusual incident. Biographies are admittedly scant but with so many great players it would have proved difficult to give due prominence to all the achievements our favourites have managed without doubling the size of the book.

Each heading is a separate reference pulling together strands surrounding the subject in question in a style which I hope will give the reader everything they wish to know about a particular aspect of the club without being too repetitive. In some instances a reiteration of information has been necessary but this does not happen too often.

Come on you mighty Reds

Darren Phillips, Heywood, Autumn 2003

Foreword

Few would dispute that the good times have returned to Anfield and with them the profile of the club has raised to even greater heights. This was always the way it had been during my time on the Anfield playing staff and seems to have been the case for as long as I can remember.

Those of us lucky enough to play professional football realise not just the importance but the sheer weight of history to our clubs. This is certainly true of all Liverpool players as it's the very foundation all our achievements were built on and measured against. No player ever forgot that and we were determined to live up to in order to write our own chapters of yet more glorious history.

All these are chronicled in this book along with the contributions of those who are not so well or even fondly remembered.

I congratulate the author on using an entertaining format to convert many aspects of Liverpool's rich history which not only sums up the player or event in a nutshell but also allows the reader to either dive in and read from cover to cover or nip in to receive all the information they require in bit sized chunks. Either way it is both a pleasurable and enlightening book which will appeal to a wide range of fans and which I can heartily recommend to all Reds no matter what their age or knowledge of the team.

The pride I draw from our club's traditions only mirrors the joy I feel in turning out for Liverpool. I hope reading this book provides all our fans with similar inspiration.

Acknowledgments

The author may shove his name on the front of a book but without the help and genuine understanding of others there is every chance the book shelves would be empty. The thank yous you are about to read are both heartfelt and appreciated.

As usual I reserve the biggest amount of appreciation possible to my wife Donna and children Sophie and Sam. They are the power behind everything I do and the spur I use to achieve more. They are the ones who have put up with me hogging the computer screen while their computer needs took a back seat. On a serious note without their love and support I'd find what I do a whole lot more difficult. I love the three of you to bits. Right up to the sky and back down again.

Sincere thanks to Eddie Cotton for supplying most of the reference books I've used. Such a noble act considering the length of time I usually hold on to the stuff. I promise you mate that if you haven't got them back by the time this book comes out it won't be too long after. Feet up and a nice cup of tea with this one I reckon.

Photographs are supplied by kind permission of the Association of Sports Photographers with copyright owned by George Herringshaw and Sporting-Heroes.net who can also be found on the internet at www.sporting-heroes.net and shol.co.uk. My thanks go to ASP and the photographers who took the photographs. Stuart Franklin, Nigel French and George Herringshaw.

Thanks to Aureus Publishing for bringing this book to you. Thanks to each and every player, official and fan of this great club. Without their contributions over the past century and more there would be nothing to write about.

A

Gary Ablett

Gary Ablett became an undeserved scapegoat for The Reds poor run during the early 1990s. He seemed to be a worthy successor to the many defensive mantels that had gone before him. Making his debut just before Christmas 1986 as a deputy for Alan Hansen he returned to the starting XI for the final few games of the season this time managing to score in a 3-0 win over Nottingham Forest in the opening game of that run. Chances were limited the following season but a League Championship winners' medal was a fair reward for his contribution. The 1988-89 campaign saw him establish himself as a first choice in the number 2 shirt. Liverpool signed a number of fine defenders over the intervening years but, injury apart, Ablett continued to figure regularly attracting the attention of other clubs - approaches that were flatly refused as he continued to operate in every position across the backline.

However, after almost 10 years at Anfield since signing as a trainee Gary was allowed to join Everton in January 1992 for £750,000. His last months at the club were turbulent. The Reds were all at sea defensively and most fingers were pointed at the young Scouser when asked to identify the weakest link. It was a disappointing ending to a career which seemed to have so much more to offer. After a few seasons at Goodison Park Birmingham City recruited Ablett to aid their push for a Premier League place but their failure ensured there was no return to the top flight and after being released in January 2001 due to persistent injury problems he teamed up with old Anfield colleague Steve McMahon at Blackpool on a short term contract.

Alan A'Court

One of the finest wingers in Liverpool's recent history has more than a fair shout of being labelled as an Anfield great and would have come to the fore far sooner than he did had he not been competing with Billy Liddell for his place in the side. There was no shifting the legendary flanker unless he was either injured which rarely happened, switched to the right or was selected to lead the forward line. The knock on effects of Louis Bimpson's absence allowed A'Court his chance during the 1954-55 season Liverpool's first back in the second division when he played more games than he had managed in the previous two campaigns since his first selection in February 1953.

Defenders at any level would have found it difficult to cope with the Rainhill born player who combined speed with great crossing and set up many chances for others. However, his prowess was not limited to providing goals. Like Billy Liddell he packed a mighty shot and while 63 goals from 382 career games for The Reds was less of a return than other wingers it was still a creditable goals to games ratio. Despite playing outside the top flight he did enough to come to the attention of the England selectors who awarded him a first cap against Northern Ireland in November 1957. England lost the game 3-2 but A'Court scored and did enough to convince the powers that be that he should become part of the contingent that made their way to Sweden the following summer for the World Cup Finals. Alan made appearances against Brazil, Austria and the USSR but couldn't help avoid an early flight home for his country. He made one more outing in an England shirt before the standards set by a young Bobby Charlton became too much to match.

By this time he could legitimately call the left side of midfield his own at club level and after eight seasons he played a huge part in Liverpool's return to the First Division. He was an ever present during that term but lost his place to Kevin Lewis just before Christmas 1962 making just a few more appearances towards the end of the season. He missed the next campaign thereby missing out on a championship medal and managed just one more outing in the 2nd leg of the European Cup preliminary tie with KR Reykjavik before trying his luck with Tranmere Rovers. He retired at the close of the 1965-66 season but took coaching positions at Norwich City, Chesterfield, Crewe Alexandra, Chester and Stoke City before taking a temporary assignment in the Southern African republic of Zambia.

John Aldridge

For the native scouser who started his professional career with Newport County signing for Liverpool was a dream come true. The fans always welcomed him before his recruitment from Oxford United with chants of "Aldridge is a Kopite." Aldo is and always will be a Kopite. A warm reception is always guaranteed for the former Tranmere Rovers boss who finished his stay at Anfield in September 1990 after scoring 61 goals from 102 games. His last strike for the club was the sixth in the 9-0 demolition of Crystal Palace - a penalty scored with his first touch after coming on as a substitute.

Real Sociedad was his next port of call before returning 'home' for Prenton Park. Initially signed as a player he became team manager within a few seasons and carried on his outstanding scoring exploits before deciding to play only when necessary. Although appearances eventually became few and far between, he was still no stranger to the scoresheet. After retiring he had the chance to concentrate on full-time management and getting Tranmere into the Premier League but despite taking the Wirral-based side to the Worthington Cup Final in 2000 and maintaining an excellent record in the cups he resigned in March 2001 with Rovers adrift at the bottom of Division One.

John Aldridge. A Kopite who saw his dream come true when he signed for his beloved Reds in February 1987 from Oxford United. He was at the forefront of the Liverpool side which swept all before them during the 1987-88 season. He left to join Real Sociedad two seasons later following the return of Ian Rush from Juventus.

Anfield

Although Liverpool Football Club and Anfield are renowned names in the football world Everton were the first team to call the stadium home. Only when a row over the rental of the ground came to a head in 1892 did the club move away. Consequently the stadium had no team. Landowner John Houlding decided to form his own club. After being told that he could not retain the name Everton he opted for Liverpool. It cost him £6000 to buy the land.

The stadium's first competitive game saw Everton beat Earlestown 5-0 on September 28th 1884. Liverpool's debut came in a friendly with Rotherham United on 1st September 1892. The Yorkshiremen found themselves on the wrong end of a 7-1 scoreline. Two days later Higher Walton were thrashed 8-0 in the Lancashire League. Liverpool's first Football League game at Anfield came on 9th September 1893 when Lincoln City were soundly beaten 4-0.

Anfield has hosted a number of international games and its fair share of other sporting events. Tennis was played during the war years at which time the legendary Fred Perry graced the field. Boxing bouts were regular sights for many years. Rugby League and Union games have featured heavily in recent years. Anfield was used for a football 'B' international in 1995 and until the latter stages of Euro 96 for three group games involving Italy, The Czech Republic and Russia plus a quarter-final tie between France and Holland. Anfield held the first of six international matches as far back as 1889 when England beat Ireland 6-1. Further England games took place in 1905, 1922, 1926, 1931 and 2001. The ground has also been used as a neutral venue for games involving other home nations.

The controversial eliminator for the 1978 World Cup finals between Scotland and Wales was played at Anfield in October 1977. Scotland won 2-0 and Kenny Dalglish scored with a flicked header, but the tie was made safe for The Scots after a penalty was awarded for handball. TV replays seemed to suggest that the hand making contact was that of Joe Jordan.

Holland and The Republic of Ireland played a qualifying game for Euro 96. The Dutch eased their way through 2-0 in December 1995. Five FA Cup semi-finals have been contested on the ground. Italy returned in September 1998 to take on Wales in a European Championships qualifier. Nine months later The Welsh returned to play Denmark. In both games Wales lost 2-0.

After 109 years The Liverpool board mooted the possibility of moving from their famous stadium and building a new ground just 400 yards away or moving to another part of the city.

Anfield - in full flow during another domestic victory for the Reds

The Anfield Road End

The usual mixture of timber and corrugated iron were the base elements of the stand built on the Anfield Road end of the ground. The original structure remained largely untouched until 1965 when slight alterations and improvements were carried out. It eventually became the designated area for away fans to watch their team and had seats installed for the home supporters in 1982. The visitors' area became a small terraced pen in the corner of the stand with seating only provided when teams with a huge support were due to play.

The small terraced area was renovated as a result of The Taylor Report in the early 1990's. After much negotiation and planning a second tier was built on the stand and is the most recent major improvement to be made to the ground.

Appearances

Ian Callaghan's 843 games is a tally which will take some beating. In fact post-Bosman and with freedom of contract there is some likelihood that it will never be bettered. 15 seasons of consistency is the benchmark any player would need to meet. The top ten appearance makers for the club in all League and Cup games are:

1	Ian Callaghan	843(5)
2	Emlyn Hughes	657
3	Ray Clemence	656
4	Phil Neal	653 (2)
5	Tommy Smith	632 (1)
6	Ian Rush	621 (28)
7	Bruce Grobbelaar	610
8	Alan Hansen	603 (4)
9	Chris Lawler	546
10	Billy Liddell	536

Appearances as a substitute are in brackets

Many players have turned out for the club just once. Of that number Howard Kaye can consider himself particularly unlucky. He played over 150 times during the Second World War but as all these games were outside the Football League/FA structure he only ever made one official appearance - in a 3-2 home defeat to Blackpool in April 1947. Some players didn't even get the chance of 90 minutes in a red shirt.

Kevin Kewley's only chance to grab the limelight came when he replaced Terry McDermott in a home league game with Middlesbrough in 1978. The Reds ran out 2-0 winners but Kewley never appeared on the team sheet again and had his contract cancelled soon after that game. Given the striking talent at Anfield during the mid to late '80's reserve striker John Durnin had his work cut out trying to break into the first team but was given little chance to prove his worth on his only opportunity. The 4th Round Littlewoods Cup tie at Upton Park was a forgone conclusion by the time he was introduced. The match finished 4-1 to West Ham United.

Joe Dines is another who only managed one game for the club despite playing in 27 amateur internationals and winning a gold medal in the 1912 Olympic Games.

Colin Russell made his only showing as a substitute in a disappointing 1-0 home defeat to Sunderland at the tail end of the 1980-81 campaign. Keith Burkenshaw made his only appearance for The Reds towards the latter part of the 1954-55 campaign and was sold soon after. However, that didn't stop him making a successful career at West Bromwich Albion and other clubs.

Attendances

Anfield's largest crowd came in a 4th Round FA Cup tie on 2nd February 1952. 61,905 people crammed into the ground to see The Reds triumph 2-1 over Wolves. Although precise figures are difficult to find the lowest league crowd at Anfield was approximately 1000 for a Second Division game against Loughborough in December 1895.

B

Phil Babb

The summer of 1994 proved a pivotal time in the career of Phil Babb. While a number of British players were resting on hot sunny beaches the Coventry City defender was on World Cup duty with The Republic of Ireland. A £3.75 million transfer to Liverpool was the reward for his distinguished performances in the USA. Bought to form part of the sweeper system operated during the 1994-95 season he initially didn't prosper as well as he may have wished. 4-4-2 was his preferred format as it allowed him the freedom to roam forward and was a role in which he had clearly excelled for both club and country. His control and passing were criticised as a result although these deficiencies were out-weighed by his other qualities.

A League Cup winners medal was the reward for his endeavours in that first season at Anfield but injury struck during the following campaign and although he made a return in place of Neil Ruddock, worries about his fitness continued. Liverpool readopted the 4-4-2 system and while he came to greater prominence in the team, the worries of his early form still seemed foremost in his mind. He dropped out of the Anfield limelight and after some time in the reserves inter-rupted by a loan to Tranmere Rovers he departed for Sporting Lisbon.

Jack Balmer

Despite being the nephew of two Everton players Jack Balmer is one of the most celebrated names ever to wear a red shirt. He started as an amateur at Goodison Park but moved to Liverpool in 1935. He stayed at Anfield until 1952 yet his career was limited to just 12 playing seasons due to the Second World War. During the war years he still turned out for Liverpool and even won unofficial international honours.

His greatest hour has to be scoring three consecutive hat-tricks in league games. No other Liverpool player scored during the 3-0 victory over Portsmouth, the 4-1 win against Derby County and the 4-2 thriller with Arsenal.

The Bargain Basement

Newspaper headlines will very often scream about how exorbitant a player's fee may be and question whether he will be worth the money invested in him. This can't happen when a player is picked up for what can only be described as a snip. Recruits from this canny area of the transfer market include some of the club's all time greats. Ray Clemence attracted a modest £20,000 fee in 1967. His old club Scunthorpe United also supplied the talents of Kevin Keegan. His transfer earned them another £35,000 which by any standards was a reasonably priced acquisition.

Liverpool's buying policy over many years was one of extreme prudence which may go some way to explaining why there have been so many highly skilled but low priced players appearing for the club. Before Ian St John's arrival in 1961 the Anfield board had never seen fit to spend more than £15,000 - both Kevin Lewis and Gordon Milne arrived for that fee shortly before St John's capture. The princely sum of £75 was exchanged with Preston North End for Jimmy Ross in 1894 and set a mark which wasn't exceeded for some years.

The Reds' first big money splash was the purchase of Jimmy Smith who earned Ayr United £5,000 in 1929. A year later Tom Bradshaw became the next bank buster. Bury accepted a £9,000 bid which was the third highest fee ever paid. Before 1961 only Albert Subbins' £13,000 transfer fee in 1946 was greater.

John Barnes

When he signed for Liverpool John Barnes was still a couple of months away from his 24th birthday. Most thought he was an awful lot older - a consequence of building a fine reputation at an early age. After nearly 300 appearances for Watford a move to a bigger club was inevitable. Rumour was that Barnes was more keen on a move abroad than linking up with another English club, even if that club was of the stature of Liverpool.

Whatever the rights or wrongs of that claim Barnes put pen to paper in the summer of 1987 and set the foundations for a glorious stay at the club. When he linked up once more with Kenny Dalglish at Newcastle United it really did mark the end an era. Barnes was the last member of this squad to leave the club. His near 10 year stay was one of distinction and laden with honours - both for the club and individually. League Championships, FA and League Cup medals plus two Player of the Year Awards are testament to that. In days of multi-million pound fees for nothing short of ordinary players the £900,000 that brought him to Anfield looks paltry. After retiring he took up the job of chief coach at Celtic, again under the watchful eye of Kenny Dalglish who was the Director of Football at Parkhead. The role ended abruptly with the Glasgow giants struggling to keep pace with Rangers and after a humiliating defeat to Inverness Caledonian Thistle in the Scottish FA Cup.

*John Barnes - A mercurial winger who seemed one the most unlikely Liverpool players on the surface
showed just what he could contribute to a team throughout his Anfield career. An instant hit with the fans
he left after just under a decade after arriving to link up once more with the man who brought him to
Merseyside, Kenny Dalglish.*

Kevin Baron

Preston North End have supplied Liverpool with many players over their history. One of these was inside forward Kevin Baron who joined The Reds following the Second World War and despite standing just 5'6" tall proved more than a handful for opposing defenders. He made his official debut in the FA Cup which resumed before the Football League reconvened. Liverpool won the first post-war championship but Baron remained in the reserves making just 12 outings over the following two seasons.

With the second string he had lifted the 1948-49 Central League title finally earning himself an extended run when the new season kicked off. He remained in the picture all season playing in the 1950 FA Cup final but saw Phil Taylor and others limit his chances throughout the 1950-51 season. He missed just two games the following season and scored 10 goals from just 27 games the following season. He remained on the fringes of the side until May 1954 when he joined Southend United. Latterly he played for Northampton Town and Aldershot. In between those two engagements he dropped out of the Football League to play for Wisbech. He died in 1971, just over a decade after retiring.

Harold Barton

Though a player at home on either wing he undoubtedly enjoyed taking the right flank during his five seasons with The Reds. From this berth he provided many goals for the prolific Gordon Hodgson and Jimmy Smith during the early 1930s. Quick and skilful Barton will always be noted for his part in the 7-4 win over Everton in February 1933 when he scored a hat-trick from the wing. That season was by far his best in front of goal with 13 strikes from 34 league games.

His strike rate in the FA Cup is almost one for each of the six games he played. It should be pointed out that the four goals he managed to notch in the competition were in the same match a few weeks before that infamous Derby clash. Chesterfield entertained Liverpool in the 4th Round and found themselves three goals adrift by the break. Barton had claimed the lot. The Spireites rallied to pull two back but Barton managed to hit one more and ease Liverpool through to the next stage.

A stay which began with spells in and out of the first XI ended with the preference for Berry Nieuwenhuys and others. Three seasons as an instant first choice had helped him amass just over a century of appearances for the club.

Peter Beardsley

£1.9 million made this unassuming Geordie domestic football's record buy in July 1988. He more than proved his worth in his first season and for a few more beyond. Despite a fairly inauspicious start his departure just before the 1990-91 season kicked off caused a few shock waves among the fans and not only because he made the short journey across Stanley Park.

Many thought he shouldn't have been shown the exit door so quickly, especially at a time of rebuilding when experienced heads were vital. For a player with far more creative urges than an out-and-out goal scorer he totalled

Peter Beardsley - A world class forward who spent the best four years of his career with Liverpool and proved a worthy successor to Kenny Dalglish in the number 7 shirt.

45 strikes from 136 full appearances. Before joining Liverpool he had been at Carlisle United, Newcastle United and Vancouver Whitecaps. Manchester United took a look at him during a trial while he was in Vancouver but the Old Trafford manager decided not to pursue his interest. His time in Canada ended soon after with Peter returning to the North East.

Kevin Keegan brought him back to St James Park for a £1 million ending a moderate time at Goodison Park as they pushed to become Premier League champions but The Magpies failed to make the final leap. On Keegan's departure Beardsley spent short spells at Manchester City and Bolton Wanderers. When Keegan joined Fulham Beardsley was one of the first names he looked to sign. The Cottagers sought to achieve promotion to the First Division and once the job was done Peter was on his travels once more, this time to Hartlepool United where he finished his professional career. A stint as part of the England coaching set up ended with the resignation of his long time mentor Kevin Keegan in October 2000.

He has recently spent time coaching Middlesbrough's youth players but was offered another return to St James Park by Bobby Robson in a similar capacity to the one that he enjoyed at The Riverside.

Reuben Bennett

The fact that Liverpool's backroom team remained one of the most modest coaching outfits in the game for many years hasn't stopped their contributions being brought into the open. If there is a man who could be considered to be something of an unsung hero, that man is Reuben Bennett. He joined The Reds' set up in November 1958 after successful coaching and managerial spells north of the border. A goalkeeper of some repute he hung up his gloves eight years before arriving at Anfield after spells with Hull City, Queen of the South and Dundee. The war took a chunk out of his professional career but he doubled up his service by acting as an army physical training instructor.

Dundee saw his promise and offered him the chance to extend his association with the club by utilising his expertise in training and fitness. Three years later he was appointed as Ayr United's manager before moving on to Motherwell and Third Lanark. It was with Lanark that he first worked with a Shankly. Bill's elder brother Bob. The two played a major role in their club regaining their place among the elite of the Scottish game.

Whether Bill asked his sibling for a reference about Bennett will probably remain unknown but Shanks was keen to hold on each member of staff he had inherited when taking the Liverpool job in December 1959. His methods just like his manager's were rigorous and designed to ensure the players were fully equipped to deal with the demands of a long and arduous season. Even when he had officially retired as a coach in 1971 to take up a scouting role he continued to put the players through their paces during running exercises and carried on well into his 60s.

He played no part in affairs from the mid to late 1980s but remained a regular on matchdays after his retirement. His enthusiasm for training and working to help Liverpool Football Club stay as a force never waned until his untimely death in December 1989 at the age of 75.

Patrik Berger

A stylish midfielder who started his career at Slavia Prague before moving to Borussia Dortmund whom he joined within three seasons of entering professional ranks. Already capped a number of times by the Czech Republic he came to prominence during his country's run to the final of Euro 96. There were a list of possible suitors keen to sign him but Liverpool, the team he supported as a boy, swooped with a £3.25 million bid.

That he turned his back on a chance to play in the Champions League with Dortmund was seen as a measure of his eagerness to join The Reds. The German side went on to lift the European Cup with a 3-1 win over Juventus. Collectively Liverpool's season hit no such heights but Berger endeared himself to the fans who were expecting to see the silky skills with explosive thrust in the last third of the field. A moderate start to his Anfield career was turned round when he appeared as a second half replacement for Stan Collymore in an away fixture against Leicester City. The game was meandering towards a goalless draw before the Czech took control of its destiny single-handedly. The Leicester defenders found his pace and control too much to cope with as he scored a couple of sensational goals in a 3-0 win. The following week, in a full appearance, he repeated the trick against Chelsea.

Roy Evans was a great fan of the player but found himself leaving Patrik out of the squad more often than he played him during the 1997-98 season prompting interest from a host of clubs. Liverpool had more than their fair share of midfielders especially of a creative nature at the time and they all had similar qualities and abilities. The player was quoted as being ready and willing to leave with Benfica cast as front runners especially having just recruited his great friend from the international scene Karol Poborsky. But Liverpool point blank refused to talk business and eventually Berger was reintegrated back into the side. A first team regular for the 2000-01 season he lost his place in the side as a result of a serious knee injury suffered during Liverpool's 4-3 defeat at Elland Road in November. Early forecasts had him sidelined for the remainder of the campaign but after pioneering surgery in America he managed to return to the fray for the last few weeks of the season making a significant contribution to the FA and UEFA Cup wins after being introduced as a substitute. However, a sustained run outside the first team partly caused by injury saw him feature rarely until his contract expired in the summer of 2003.

Stig Inge Bjornbye

Norwegian champions Rosenberg made a handsome profit on the player they had picked up from lower ranking Kongsvinger. He had spent a little time out of the first team, but when asked to step up he disappointed no one.

In December 1992 he impressed Liverpool boss Graeme Souness so much that he put in a £600,000 bid for his services. A commanding display for Norway against England, which put paid to their European Nation's Cup bid in the summer, contributed to this interest. Injury to David Burrows was another contributing factor to his arrival. He found his first season tough going. The quick fire style of the English game seemed to have him stretched to the limit but within a couple of seasons he displayed the type of form and style of play which fitted perfectly into the style required by newly appointed manager Roy Evans. Stig epitomised just what the Liverpool boss was asking his full-backs to achieve. Combining well with his midfield partner he would undertake countless overlaps and was able to deliver delicious balls into the area for attackers which seemed to have been so well delivered that he could not have placed them better with his hand. He was equally strong in his defensive duties although proved himself prone to the occasional gaffe in both areas of the field.

A broken leg suffered towards the close of the 1994-95 season forced him out of the line-up and when he returned to fitness he found his replacements had been in such outstanding form that he had to wait before claiming back his place. He remained in and out of the side for almost three seasons before joining Blackburn.

Bogey Teams

Despite beating the best Europe and the world has to offer there have always been teams that The Reds cannot seem to conquer. In the 1960's it was Leicester City. The Foxes were firmly established in the top flight when Liverpool achieved promotion in 1962. Of the first six league meetings after that The Reds won just once. Leicester won the 1963 FA Cup semi-final tie between the two clubs when Gordon Banks was in great form. The Midlanders' fortunes slid soon after as they fell to the lower echelons of the league structure. They returned in 1981 and ended Liverpool's unbeaten home run of 85 matches.

Brighton have proved a thorn in The Reds' side especially in the cups. They met Liverpool in successive seasons: 1982-83 and 1983-84. Former player Jimmy Melia was managing the south coast side who made it all the way to Wembley after the first meeting. Another Liverpool old boy, Jimmy Case, sealed a 2-1 5th round win at Anfield. A year later and one round earlier only the venue changed as Brighton cruised to a 2-0 home win. Liverpool have met The Seagulls since that time and have secured easy wins.

The Boot Room

The inner sanctum of many Liverpool managerial teams throughout the years is the boot room. The infamous cubby hole stood in a corridor of the Main Stand. Bill Shankly's reign is generally accepted to be the origins of what is now viewed as the Anfield tradition of the coaching staff getting together and chewing over team affairs.

When a manager decided to leave the club there would be no conjecture as to which big name might replace him. It was generally accepted that one of the unassuming deputies would step into the breach and maintain the seamless running of the well oiled red machine.

The boot room was exactly what it sounds like. A small room with football boots covering its walls. A select group of opposition managers may be invited in to share a tot of whisky or two following a game but a closed door policy operated in respect of everyone bar the boot room staff themselves. Each and every would-be visitor had to knock before gaining admittance which, in most cases would be denied. The actual boot room was pulled down during Graeme Souness' highly controversial reign to make more office space. It now only exists as a byword for managerial excellence and loyalty. The Liverpool back room boys have proved to be some of the most devoted servants to the game.

Many from their number have stayed at Anfield for a generation, some for a working lifetime. Albert Shelly joined the club before the Second World War and served the Reds for almost 30 years. He was seen as one of the best physios of his day. Other long servers include Bob Paisley, Joe Fagan, Ronnie Moran, Rueben Bennet, Tom Saunders and John Bennison. Bennison worked closely with Tom Saunders overseeing the club's youth players for over 20 years and was another who had never played professional football yet enjoyed an amateur career.

Former players that have been made members of the backroom team include Chris Lawler who took charge of the reserves from 1983 to 1986. Phil Thompson was appointed to the same post by Kenny Dalglish, and held the job until Graeme Souness decided to recruit Sammy Lee in 1992. Phil Thompson returned to the club as Assistant Manager to Houllier when the Frenchman took sole charge of team affairs in November 1998.

Although not a part of the 'classic' bootroom tradition which most observers reckon ended with the arrival of Graeme Souness, Phil Boersma is another Anfield old boy who returned to play a role. He arrived as part of the deal which Souness brokered when returning to the club as Assistant Manager and eventually as physio.

Scouting duties have been assumed by Geoff Twentyman who was appointed chief scout in 1967. Twentyman was a star of Liverpool's side during the 1950s but was replaced by Ron Yeats in 1986 who was brought back to the club by Kenny Dalglish. Twentyman took up a similar role with Graeme Souness at Glasgow Rangers. Yeats has remained in the post ever since.

Doug Livermore was recruited by Roy Evans when he took charge in 1994 to assist with first team duties. He had played no more than 14 times for The Reds during his four years at the club spanning the late 1960s and early 1970s before he was allowed to leave. After retiring as a player he undertook coaching duties with Cardiff City, Swansea City, Norwich City and Tottenham Hotspur as well as serving as Assistant Manager to the Welsh National side. He left the club along with Roy Evans in November 1998 when the joint-manager experiment was ended.

The Bosman Ruling

When the little known Belgian footballer Jon Marc Bosman took his contract dispute to the European Courts of Justice very few people, in or outside the game could have realised the impact the eventual decision would have. The well documented ramifications of his complaint now ensures that any player who comes out of contract can negotiate a deal with another club; the team he is leaving is not entitled to any transfer fee whatsoever. In addition, should six months or less of the player's existing contract remain he is then free to sign an agreement to join a foreign club once that contract has finally expired. As no transfer fee is involved the player can negotiate a bumper pay day - usually up to the value of any estimated transfer fee. Notable signings under the arrangement are Steve Staunton (the first player to join from another English club), Erik Meijer, Marcus Babbel, Pegguy Arphexad and Gary McAllister.

Steve MacManaman is the biggest name to leave the club under the ruling. He joined Real Madrid in the Summer of 1999. Others to leave under the arrangement include reserve striker Lee Jones who joined Tranmere Rovers.

James Bradley

Stoke had nurtured the talents of midfielder James Bradley but parted company with the player when an offer came in from Liverpool in 1905. The Reds were looking to re-establish themselves following their championship win four years earlier. That the title returned to Anfield at the close of the campaign was in no small part down to the industry of Bradley and others after a moderate start to the new season. A gifted passer with what the modern game now describes as vision managed to settle the men around him down and richly deserved the reward he and others earned. Tom Watson refused to look much further than him for another four seasons but eventually gave John McConnell an extended run in the side early in the 1910-11 campaign. The player sought pastures new not long after and moved to Reading.

Harry Bradshaw

A versatile frontman who could either lead the attack or play at outside left or right with equal aplomb. Bradshaw was the man who scored the goal which secured Liverpool's first promotion to the top flight. That goal was one of the 10 he managed from 18 games after joining from Northwich Victoria in October 1893. He also scored on debut in a 5-0 hammering of Woolwich Arsenal. Although Liverpool finished bottom of the table the following season it was a good campaign for Bradshaw on a personal level as he notched 17 goals from the 30 games he played. Relegation couldn't blunt his goalscoring. He turned in a creditable 12 strikes during the 1895-96 season when he earned the last of his two 2nd Division Championship medals. The first was claimed at the close of the 1893-94 campaign.

Heavily built and strong he was at the tail end of his career when he arrived on Merseyside but still showed enough promise to secure his only England cap in 1897. A year later he moved to Tottenham Hotspur and in turn to Thames Ironworks (West Ham United) both of the Southern League. A great servant to the club in its early years he made in excess of 100 appearances. Tragically, illness ended his short life on Christmas Day 1899 aged just 26. On the same day Liverpool played Derby County losing 3-2 at The Baseball Ground.

Tom Bradshaw

It took the usually spendthrift Liverpool board a record £8000 fee to tempt the man nicknamed 'Tiny' from Bury in 1930 and while the amount of money changing hands may not sound impressive it should be borne in mind that it was the fourth biggest deal in English history at the time. Although known as Tiny throughout the game Tom was anything but small.

He was an immense man in terms of stature and build with shoulders and neck that would please a heavyweight boxer. By virtue of this and his comfort on the ball he proved one of the most difficult centre backs for any striker to beat.

Despite his form he failed to win international caps during his time at Liverpool making his one and only appearance for Scotland in the infamous win over England at Wembley in 1928. That team became known as the 'Wembley Wizards' but Bradshaw only got to practice his magic at club level from then on due to the sheer competition for places at half-back.

He made almost 300 appearances for Liverpool scoring three times in the league and once in the cup. All his league goals came during the 1932-33 season. His first came in an incident packed match with Newcastle United at St James Park. The Magpies had raced to a 3-0 half-time lead but Liverpool managed to hit back just after the interval with a Gordon Hodgson penalty and a Crawford goal 10 minutes later. Crawford was drafted in for the first seven games of the season and scored four goals but strangely never figured again in Liverpool's plans. Bradshaw notched the third but the home side managed to snatch another to take the points.

However, it was at the other end of the field that The Reds got most productivity out of Tom who remained first choice until the close of the 1936-37 season. He started two of the first three games played the following year but eventually dropped out of the picture. A number of players were tried in his position that season but he never made it back and returned to his native Scotland in the new year with Third Lanark. He returned to England to take a scouting role with Norwich once his playing days were over.

David Burrows

There were high hopes for David Burrows at Anfield and justifiably so. A rising young star viewed as one of the best juniors in the country was secured for £500,000 and instantly likened to one of his new colleagues Steve Nicol. In his five years at the club he only allowed himself to shine briefly and for intermittent periods. Another drawback was a hatred of being beaten. A good habit for a player to get in to but bad when he allowed it to boil over into aggressive and rash tackles which more often than not landed him in hot water.

A spell in the reserves seemed to coincide with some of these excesses but it wasn't too long before Burrows returned. From the 1989-90 season until the close of the 1992-93 campaign he was a regular even if it was in a variety of positions including midfield and during a period when Liverpool suffered chronic injury set backs. Not that these were the only factors allowing his chance. League Championship and FA Cup Winners medals were deserved rewards even if he seemed to make little progress and still seemed a good way short of coming up to the standards of a player like Nicol. In January 1994 after almost 200 games and three rasping goals for the club he, along with Mike Marsh, was allowed to leave for West Ham United in part exchange for their left-back Julian Dicks.

Matt Busby

But for a commitment to manage Manchester United this footballing legend could have taken the Anfield hotseat as the job was offered to him. However, it is worth reflecting that if he had been in a position to accept, his great friend Bill Shankly may never have become manager. Busby was another Liverpool player who fell victim to the war years and saw his Anfield career limited to a mere four seasons. From that first selection in 1936 only injury robbed him of a berth in defence. The club captaincy was bestowed on him shortly before war broke out. A handful of games capped his Liverpool career but it was during this time that the idea of putting him in charge of team affairs was first mooted. The Reds' directors resisted United's approach but the then Chairman Billy McConnell was instrumental in persuading his colleagues to let him go. His untimely death in 1994 was met by accolades throughout the game.

Gerry Byrne

A talented youngster who, despite making the Liverpool schoolboys squad, was nothing more than a fringe player at Anfield. He was initially rejected by Liverpool and so worked in a lead factory until he finally made the grade and signed for the club at 17. Ronnie Moran kept him out of the first team squad. He was the club captain and first choice at left-back. When Bill Shankly arrived at Anfield in December 1959 Byrne was transfer listed. He had only been given the one chance and unfortunately that came in a 5-1 defeat at Charlton. To make matters worse Gerry had scored an own-goal. Shank's gave him a further opportunity towards the end of his first season at the helm. Although asked to turn out in an alien role - right back - he must have acquitted himself well as the 1960-61 saw him become not just a first team regular but the first choice option. He played in every game of the promotion season of 1961-62.

The 1965 FA Cup Final showed his heroic qualities as he played close to the full 90 minutes with not only a gashed shin but a broken collarbone. Many players would have been inhibited by this but not Gerry. With his arm tucked beneath his jersey he played a blinder and even sent in the cross which set up Liverpool's first goal.

A few days later a home game against Inter Milan in the European Cup semi-final first leg took place. Always looking for the psychological edge Bill Shankly sent Byrne out, sling draped around his neck along with another injury victim Gordon Milne. The two paraded the FA Cup in front of The Kop. The noise level shot through the roof and played no small part in Liverpool's infamous 3-1 win. The FA Cup final heroics proved not to be a one-off. A year later in a Cup Winners' Cup tie against Celtic Byrne dislocated an elbow. The club doctor twisted it back into position and he carried on with the game.

Little wonder that Shanks described him as the toughest player he had ever seen. He was a tough tackler and exulted in the well earned nickname of Gerry the Crunch. Not that he was a dirty player. Far from it. He was only booked once during his Liverpool career and that was for querying a throw-in! He retired in 1969 but despite a briefly held coaching role has resisted the temptation to get actively involved with the game.

C

Ian Callaghan

Cally is the only player whose career spanned the years in which Liverpool transformed themselves from nothing more than second division also rans to European Champions and a world force. He also holds the record for the greatest number of appearances for the club. He turned out 848 times in all competitions including five games as a substitute. His debut in a 4-0 home win over Bristol Rovers earned him rave reviews and although many famous names graced the pitch that afternoon they all lined up once the 90 minutes were over to applaud the 17 year old debutante off the field.

Despite 19 seasons with the club his honours, at least by recent standards, seem pretty modest. Still, five championships, two FA Cup, a couple of UEFA Cup and a European Cup winners' medals are some haul. In 1974 he was

Ian Callaghan - Holder of Liverpool's record for the number of appearances.
His career spanned The Reds' days as 2nd Division also rans to the European
Cup win of 1977.

voted The Football Writers' Player of the Year. He won four England caps including two at the twilight of his playing days in 1978.

That was at the grand age of 35. Twelve years earlier he had turned out in the group stages of England's glorious 1966 World Cup campaign. This loyal servant was given a free transfer to Swansea City. After a brief stay in South Wales it was on to Cork United, Soudifjord (Norway) and Crewe Alexandra.

Captains

The first captain of Liverpool Football Club was former Evertonian Andrew Hannah. He had been an important member of the old Everton and was brought back to Anfield by John Houlding after the rebels had moved out and the new club was formed. Other skippers from Liverpool's early days include Alex Raisbeck, who steered Liverpool to their first two League Championships in 1901 and 1906. With Harry Lowe injured Bob Ferguson became the first man to lead Liverpool out in an FA Cup Final in 1914. During the 1920s Walter Wadsworth, Eph Longworth and Don McKinlay all captained the team.

Although not a definitive list of each player to have skippered The Reds when the club captain has been missing through injury or suspension all the club's post-war captains are listed as follows:

Willie Fagan	1946 - 1947
Phil Taylor	1947 - 1953
Bill Jones	1953 - 1954
Billy Liddell	1954 - 1955
Ronnie Moran	1955 - 1960
Dick White	1960 - 1961
Ron Yeats	1961 - 1970
Tommy Smith	1970 - 1973
Emlyn Hughes	1973 - 1979
Phil Thompson	1979 - 1982
Graeme Souness	1982 - 1984
Phil Neal	1984 - 1985
Alan Hansen	1985 - 1988
Ronnie Whelan	1988 - 1991
Mark Wright	1991 - 1992
Ian Rush	1992 - 1996
John Barnes	1996 - 1997
Paul Ince	1997 - 1999
Jamie Redknapp	1999 - 2002
Sami Hyypia	2002 - present

Before his retirement in 1983 the Liverpool players that had won the Milk/League Cup against Manchester United insisted Bob Paisley go up the Wembley steps to pick up the trophy. It is a tradition that has come back in recent times. Vice-captain Robbie Fowler lifted the Worthington Cup at The Millennium Stadium but injured club skipper Jamie Redknapp was ushered forward to hoist the FA Cup aloft along with Fowler at the same venue two months later. Fowler had started on the bench for the game, the same position he occupied when the UEFA Cup Final kicked off four days later. By the end of the game he had been introduced by Gerard Houllier and he invited Sami Hyypia who had been given the captain's armband at the start to receive the trophy.

Jamie Carragher

Jamie Carragher has been considered something of a utility player able to give great service in midfield and when called on the centre of defence. Now he is seen as not just as a versatile player but possibly one of the best left-backs on duty over the recent seasons. A graduate of Liverpool's 1996 FA Youth Cup winning side he made his debut in January 1997 as a substitute in the League Cup defeat by Middlesbrough. Although the game didn't go The Reds' way it was clear that another gem had been unearthed via the much praised youth policy. Just over a week later he was handed his first start covering for John Barnes in a home game with Aston Villa. Within the opening 60 seconds he was booked for a petulant challenge. Minutes after the interval he notched his first goal for the club. It was the opener in a 3-0 win but the scoreline flattered The Reds who had struggled in front of goal until the new boy crashed in a header from short range.

Over the next season he was a far more regular face in the side playing in almost half the matches and winning England youth and 'B' caps in the process. His strength on the ball and in the tackle makes him a natural in any defensive position be that in a back four or a midfield holding role.

Senior international caps followed and, but for the presence of Ashley Cole, he may well have been England's first choice left-back, but three winner's medals during the 2000-2001 campaign was some reward for the player who had more than a decent shot at claiming the club's player of the year accolade.

Jimmy Case

A man who many believe was the best player never to win an England cap. Regardless of any doubters he may have had in the national squad's hierarchy he was never underestimated by Liverpool or the fans and earned more club honours than many established internationals could even dream of - four

Jimmy Case - Once voted as Europe's Best Young player Jimmy Case found it hard to cement his place in the side for a number of seasons despite his obvious potential.

league championships, three European Cups and a League cup winners medal. After seven seasons and over 250 appearances for The Reds he joined Brighton and Hove Albion in 1981. He came back to haunt his old club in the 5th round of the 1983 FA Cup by scoring a late winner in a 2-1 win for The Seagulls. That Anfield win marked the beginning of a very sticky run for Liverpool in meetings with the South Coast club. A short journey along the seaside saw him turn out for Southampton and meant he remained a regular visitor to Anfield until his retirement. A short spell as manager at The Dell ended his association with the professional game although he has turned out in a number of veterans' tournaments organised by the Professional Footballers' Association for teams representing The Reds.

Championships

Although the championship crown hasn't been to Anfield since 1990 there is very little doubt that the club's trophy cabinet is where every Liverpool fan would like to see it return. Regardless of any particular guise it may hide under to finish top of the your country's leading division is the ultimate prize. As Bill Shankly once said: "It's our bread and butter."

The Premiership is still to be won by The Reds but before its inception in 1992 Liverpool had been crowned champions 18 times. A record light years ahead of every other club. Even closest rivals Manchester United would have to claim another three title victories to draw level.

Chants

All clubs have a section of support known for its singing and chanting. But no club and no group of supporters can have achieved more acclaim than Liverpool and the world famous Kop. With few, if any exceptions everyone connected with the game has a story emanating from a visit to Anfield. Whether that is due to ruthless mickey taking, the adulation of a great, a deadpan put down of a rival or reaction to funny or momentous incidents. Liverpool fans have a response to suit any occasion.

The Charity Shield

As regular winners of the domestic game's two top honours, the League and FA Cup, Liverpool have played in a fair few of what are now pre-season curtain raisers. The first appearance came just four days after the end of the 1921-22 season. Liverpool as league champions took on FA Cup holders Huddersfield Town. The Terriers took the honours with a single goal. That match was played at Old Trafford. Liverpool's first Charity Shield showpiece at Wembley was a tempestuous affair with Leeds United. Kevin Keegan and Billy Bremner were sent off as tempers boiled. Keegan threw his shirt to the ground in disgust and frustration at his dismissal. Liverpool eventually triumphed 6-5 on penalties following a 1-1 draw over 90 minutes. Until the opening of the 2003-04 season Liverpool had played in 20 Charity Shield games winning six, losing nine and sharing the silverware on five occasions.

Phil Chisnall

Although he enjoyed a particularly average stay with Liverpool embracing a mere handful of first team games his claim to fame is being the last player to be directly transferred between Old Trafford and Anfield. His first campaign saw him start the initial two league games of the season as a replacement for the injured Ian St John. He didn't get another look in until the final four matches during which he scored his only goal for the club. Outside the Football League he made an appearance at Wembley coming on as a substitute for Alf Arrowsmith during the 1964 Charity Shield tie with West Ham. The teams shared the honours after a 2-2 draw. He had arrived at Anfield in April that year for £25,000 after playing 35 League games for United. He made his debut, and scored, in Liverpool's very first European match against Reykjavik in August 1964. During the following season he made just one appearance in the 1st leg of the Cup Winners Cup semi-final against Celtic at Parkhead in April 1966. Liverpool lost by the game's only goal but a 2-0 win in the Anfield return secured passage to the final at Hampden Park. He made no further first team appearances and he stayed at Anfield for another year before accepting a move to Southend United in the close season of 1967.

Christmas Day

These days players are allowed to spend the majority of Christmas Day with their families. With such a busy festive period it is seen as the right thing to do. However, it wasn't always this way. Up until 1958 and with very few exceptions, players up and down the country would be expected to turn out. Liverpool's last fixture on that date involved a long trek to Grimsby. The Reds lost 3-1. The Reds' last goal on Christmas Day came courtesy of Tony Rowley, a current Liverpool season ticket holder, who scored 38 goals in his 61 appearances for the club.

Ray Clemence

From the giant keeper's first appearance for Liverpool it was obvious he could provide the defensive cornerstone any great side needs. Even so it still took him two seasons to unseat Tommy Lawrence. Along with his back line he provided the rock solid wall that attackers found very difficult to break down. Defensive records were set and then bettered. He established himself as one of the best 'keepers in the country and, as a consequence England caps came in their dozens. Much is made of the fact that Peter Shilton's record 129 international appearances would have been far greater had the Liverpool number one not been on the scene. However, there is little doubt that had it not been for Shilton Clemence's tally of 67 caps would have been greater.

When he eventually left the club for Tottenham Hotspur in August 1981 he had racked up 656 appearances. After seven seasons with Spurs he joined the White Hart Lane coaching staff. Media work and the co-ordination of Barnet's fight against relegation from the Football League were sandwiched between that and his current role as England's goalkeeping supremo.

Ray Clemence

Avi Cohen

Liverpool's first Israeli international joined the club before the 1979-80 championship season. The £200,000 paid to Maccabi Tel Aviv was not a king's ransom but when compared against his early showings it seemed an excellent piece of business. Although he had just three first team starts plus one call off the subs bench in that season his contribution towards winning the championship was as notable as any ever present or goal scoring machine. The Reds entered a home game with Aston Villa needing a result to secure the title. Liverpool held a slim lead. Villa were pressing forward in search of an equaliser. It came courtesy of poor Avi Cohen who put through his own net. The despair on his face was obvious, but, in one of football's strange twists of fate he restored the lead five minutes after half time. In the end Liverpool cruised to a 4-1 win. The next term saw him replace Alan Kennedy at left back. Kennedy was having a fitful time with injury and the Israeli took his chance. His last game that season, in February, was also his last for Liverpool. His contract was cancelled in November 1981.

Stan Collymore

Perhaps the seeds of destruction Stan sowed at the tail end of his career were evident during the opening stages of his time at Anfield. The £8.5 million

Avi Cohen - Israeli defender Avi Cohen had the distinction of scoring at both ends in the 4-1 win over Aston Villa which clinched in championship in 1980. He left during the following season returning to the club he was signed from Macabbi Tel Aviv.

record signing decided to question the tactics of his manager in a magazine article and thereby started the ball rolling on a tempestuous two season stay on Merseyside.

Within an hour of his debut against Sheffield Wednesday he unleashed a thunderbolt of a shot from 20 yards after shaking off his markers. Liverpool had had their fair share of explosive players over the years but Stan seemed to be the most combustible of the lot. Injury had left him disillusioned with the club but with the Ian Rush and Robbie Fowler partnership flourishing in his absence there was no need for change. Especially given that The Reds' methodical approach to the opposition was more suited to Rush and Fowler's styles.

Injury to Rush brought Stan back into the fold and with renewed vigour he slid in a little more comfortably alongside his teammates who in turn began to play to his strengths when the right occasion arose. From his 71 starts 35 goals were a great return and begged the question - What could he have achieved had he not endured such a lean and indifferent spell?.

He continued to drift in and out of the starting XI despite some memorable games and individual performances. As a result media speculation intensified as did interest from other clubs. A boyhood Aston Villa fan Collymore decided they offered him more than Liverpool could within days of the 1996-97 season closing. Despite the £7 million fee Villa paid he was allowed to leave for a nominal amount within a few years. He retired aged 30 after a brief spell in Spain.

Colours

Liverpool may be universally known as The Reds but this hasn't been the only colour the team has played in. For the first six years of the club's existence they turned out in blue and white quarters. Red only became the 'home colours' at the start of the 1898-99 term. White shorts remained until 1964 when Bill Shankly decided the players looked far more formidable in all red. He used Ron Yeats as proof and if the record books are anything to go by it seems he had a point. The first game Liverpool played in all red was against Anderlecht in the 1964-65 European Cup. The Belgians crashed out 4-0 on aggregate after a 3-0 win at Anfield was followed by a single goal victory in the return leg.

The solid red shirts remained until 1982 at which time a fine vertical pinstripe was introduced. A change of kit manufacturer brought a return to the plain red jersey. Although the trimmings, shades and other small details underwent slight alterations it wasn't until the early 90's that stripes, this time far wider and running diagonally across the rib area, adulterated the pure red.

Away colours have been extremely varied. Until the 1980's it was usually white - either all white or with black shorts. It transformed into yellow with a red trim. For a single season during the decade it reverted to white shirts with black shorts. Then yellow once more. Since 1987 a whole host of colours and combinations have been used to avoid colour clashes.

These include silver, green, green and white. Green, white and black. Black and gold, ecru and graphite, a very vivid yellow and more recently 'turf green' with a dash of white and blue. A return to the traditional all white kit - with a dash of red- was made at the beginning of the 1998-99 campaign. The following season green with blue and white flashes were preferred. The blue was retained the for the 2000-01 season only this time with a solid panel of gold on the front and back. A new white and blue second kit which meant to be introduced for the beginning of the 2001-02 campaign was used in the first leg of the UEFA semi-final tie with Barcelona in April 2001.Black with flashes of grey and red piping was the next combination. The 2003-04 season saw a return to white jerseys this time with red trim on the chest. Black shorts were preferred.

Consistency

Consistency is a Liverpool watch word which has formed one of the many bases for The Reds' phenomenal success. Injury and suspension will very often limit the availability of squad members but in the 1965-66 championship campaign Bill Shankly used a mere 14 players over the course of the 42 game league programme. This prompted him to simply announce that he would be fielding the same team as last year when enquiries over his line ups were made. Only Geoff Strong with 21 games and one as a substitute, Alf Arrowsmith with three appearances plus two calls from the bench and Bobby Graham with a single run out in the last game of the season missed more than five games. The only other man to get a look in during the cup campaigns was Phil Chisnall who started the first leg of the European Cup Winners' Cup semi-final with Celtic at Parkhead. The club played 52 games overall.

Crewe Alexandra

There is more than a busy railway line linking Liverpool to this small Cheshire town. Many players have been exchanged between the clubs over the years. Countless loan deals have also taken effect. It was a business relationship in all but name until it was formalised in 1997. At the time the agreement which essentially meant that each club had the first right of refusal on the other's players was described as one of mutual convenience. It meant Crewe could also take players on loan with a view to not only assisting their push for the Premiership but providing Reds' youngsters with valuable first team experience.

Regular preseason friendlies have taken place but in terms of competitive fixtures Liverpool hold the upper hand. In the four league meetings The Reds have a 100% record scoring 20 goals in the process. Only one has been conceded. The story is no different in the domestic cups. Liverpool steamed to a 4-0 3rd Round victory in the only FA Cup meeting. The League Cup has seen two 2nd Round encounters. In the 1990-91 campaign Liverpool took the honours 5-1 at home and by a 4-1 margin of victory at Gresty Road.

Crossing The Park

There have been relatively few deals between Liverpool and Everton. Just 15 in nearly a century. As the table below shows there are some players who have played for both clubs but it is impossible to say whether they were transferred directly across Stanley Park or whether they were recruited from other teams. The first player to make the short trip across Stanley Park was Fred Geary who left Everton for Liverpool in 1897.

Irish international Billy Lacey made the same journey 15 years later in part exchange for Tommy Gracie and Harold Uren. In his four years at Goodison,

Lacey made 40 appearances, scoring 11 goals. While Gracie and Uren managed a combined total of 26 games for the Blues Lacey firmly established himself at Anfield making 257 appearances.

Everton's first recruit from their neighbours was Dick Forshaw. Until his departure in 1926, this highly rated forward claimed a goal every two games. His prolific scoring helped Liverpool to a couple of league championships in the early twenties. At the time he left Anfield his playing career was assumed to be in its twilight so his transfer to an emerging Everton side was widely questioned on Merseyside. The critics were soon silenced when he formed a highly effective partnership with the legendary Dixie Dean and won another championship medal in 1928.

Jimmy Payne was an exciting player. His dribbling led to favourable comparisons with Tom Finney and Stanley Matthews. Injuries blighted the latter part of his Anfield career and his eight year association with the club ended in 1956 when he joined Everton. Further injuries and a subsequent lack of confidence meant he played half a dozen games for the Blues. He retired shortly before his 30th birthday.

Tommy Johnson was in his early thirties when Everton signed him. After four years at Goodison he spent the next couple of seasons at Anfield making 39 appearances. Tony McNamara had an even shorter stay. He left Goodison in the early part of the 1957-58 season. By May 1958 he was on his way out of Merseyside and looking for another club. Although he made a meagre 11 appearances one of his three goals was on his debut in a 4-3 home win over Bristol City

Until recent seasons Liverpool hadn't made a purchase from their neighbours since 1960. It was a transfer coup which caused ripples along the Mersey. Dave Hickson, a tall and well built striker was a hero to thousands of Evertonians. His direct style was not only popular it was successful. Joining the Blues from Ellesmere Port as an 18 year old 'Dashing Dave' broke into the first team during the 1950-51 season grabbing 14 goals from 31 games and spearheading Everton's push from second division hopefuls to promotion winners in 1954. After brief spells with Aston Villa and Huddersfield. Hickson returned to Goodison in the same goal scoring form in which he left. By November 1960 he had bagged 111 goals from 243 games. A pay dispute caused him to leave The Toffees a second time. Plenty of teams expressed an interest and this time Liverpool stepped in and landed their man for £10,050. Blues' fans were speechless. A shock Liverpudlians can probably only understand by imagining Kenny Dalglish or Ian Rush signing for Everton. Hickson's stay at Anfield was a short one with 37 goals in 60 games.

Johnny Morrisey's transfer to Everton in 1962 almost caused Bill Shankly to resign his post. A £100,000 deal was struck by the Liverpool board without consultation from their manager. A repeat of which, Shanks warned, would mean his departure. Though never a goalscorer, Johnny Morrisey was a creative midfielder. He may only have played 36 times for The Reds but Shankly certainly recognised his talent. So did Blues boss Harry Catterick. In a decade at Goodison Morrisey picked up two league championships and a FA Cup Winners medal and was seen as a prime architect in constant title challenges.

Twenty years passed before the next piece of cheque book activity. David Johnson started his career at Everton as an apprentice before he was swapped for Ipswich's Rod Belfitt plus £50,000. He didn't have much time to settle at Portman Road. Liverpool made a bid of £200,000 within the year which Bobby Robson accepted. He became a first team regular in 1978-9. Partnering Kenny Dalglish in attack he won every honour in the domestic game. He also won a European Cup Winners Medal in 1981. Ian Rush's gradual emergence led to Johnson losing his place. Howard Kendall signed him in 1982 for £100,000 but when his second spell lasted just 37 games. It became clear that Liverpool had enjoyed the best Johnson had to offer.

Kendall paid a similar amount for Kevin Sheedy a few months after securing Johnson's services. In two years at Anfield the young Irishman played just three senior games. Not even his precocious skill and explosive left foot could earn him a break in a Red's midfield of Kennedy, Case, McDermott and Souness.Realising that first team opportunities would be at a premium Sheedy was transferred. Bob Paisley had reservations. Regrets which were understandable, when, in partnership with Peter Reid he drove Everton to league championship, FA Cup and European Cup Winners Cup glory in the mid-eighties.

Alan Harper, a solid performer in midfield was never a regular in this push for honours. Although he managed over 200 games in Everton colours most of his time since leaving Liverpool in 1983 was spent on the bench. He made good use of the run outs he did get and came off the bench to score the winner in the 1986 FA Cup semi-final against Sheffield Wednesday and thereby created history by setting up the first all-Merseyside final. Ironically when the cup final team was named he didn't even figure as a sub.

Peter Beardsley became an inspiration in Liverpool's near domination of the English game in the late-eighties. A £1.9m record buy Kenny Dalglish used as a lynch-pin in building a side to match those gone before. The end of Dalglish's reign saw the Geordie used less and less, by the time Graeme Souness started his first full season in charge he was rumoured to be surplus to requirements. On the eve of the 1991-92 season he was 'Blue Peter' for a price of £1m. Despite his genius Howard Kendall was unable to recapture former glories.

Gary Ablett's stay at Anfield lasted six years and began with a memorable debut goal against Nottingham Forest. Over 100 appearances for Liverpool were not enough to cement himself into the Red's defence. When the time came to leave his boyhood favourites, the short flit across the city was the option he selected. Nick Barmby defected in the summer of 2000. A Liverpool supporter as a boy Barmby decided the time was right to make the change once he heard The Reds were interested in recruiting him. The £5.5 million fee is the largest the two clubs have exchanged. Abel Xavier followed him in January 2002.

The players listed below played for both Everton and Liverpool. Some were bought direct from the other club. Those for whom this cannot be definitely said are marked with an asterix.

Tom Wyllie *
Duncan McLean *
Andrew Hannah *
Patrick Gordon *
Fred Geary
Abraham Hartley *
David Murray *
Donald Sloan *
Arthur Berry * there is some speculation as
    to whether he actually played for Everton
Harold Uren
Tommy Gracie
Bill Lacey
Frank Mitchell *

Neil McBain *
Dick Forshaw
Tom Johnson *
Jimmy Payne
Tony McNamara
Dave Hickson
John Morrissey
David Johnson
Kevin Sheedy
Peter Beardsley
Gary Ablett
Nick Barmby
Abel Xavier

Cup Winners' Cup

The one European competition Liverpool have never won and now it has been scrapped never will. The Reds' consistent qualification for the Champions Cup combined with a decidedly average record in the FA Cup mean the club has only contested the honour on five occasions. The best showing came on debut in 1966 when Liverpool made it all the way to the final after impressive victories over Juventus, Standard Leige, Honved and Glasgow Celtic. Hampden Park hosted the clash between The Reds and Borussia Dortmund.

After 90 minutes the scores were tied at 1-1 with Roger Hunt scoring for the English cup holders. Unfortunately The German side took the trophy with a winner in extra-time. The club's best showing since came in the 1996-97 season and although the 3-2 aggregate score may look tight Paris St Germaine underlined their quality during their semi-final victory.

Cups

Liverpool became only the second team to win both domestic trophies in a single season by virtue of beating the only other team to have achieved the feat in the FA Cup Final.

Arsenal were defeated 2-1 at the Millennium Stadium, the same venue where The Reds had to go to penalties to get their hands on the League Cup now known as the Worthington Cup.

Although far from the best team on the day Birmingham City pushed Liverpool all the way in the first domestic final to be held outside England and the first not be held at Wembley Stadium for over 20 years excluding replays. By picking up the UEFA Cup The Reds became the only English team ever to lift three knockout cups in the same season.

D

Kenny Dalglish

Every Liverpool fan knows the highs and lows of Kenny Dalglish's career. We all shared them with him. His lows, though seldom, were ours too and the many highs were also heartily enjoyed by millions. There is no other player who could not only replace but surpass the legacy Kevin Keegan had created. The £440,000 fee Celtic received in 1977 was a record between British clubs but one which with 14 years of hindsight appears not only modest but daylight robbery. However, Liverpool had the option of signing the teenage Kenny Dalglish over a decade previously. On 20th August 1966 he played a B team game against Southport during a fortnight's trial but failed to impress. His league debut for the club came 11 years to the day after that game against Middlesbrough. This time he scored the opener after just three minutes at Ayrsome Park.

On his second arrival at Anfield he already held a clutch of Scottish league and cup winners medals. It was a tally he set about improving south of the border and in double quick time. In his first season he nonchalantly chipped the winner in the European Cup Final win over Bruges and before he retired from active involvement in his own first team plans the honours tally boasted six league championship winners medals, three further European Cup winners medals, four League Cup Winners and one in the FA Cup.

His succession to the post of first team manager in the wake of the Heysel Stadium disaster would have proved a stern test for even the most seasoned of managers but the Scot just took it in his stride. The League and FA Cup double was a feat no Liverpool manager had achieved. Nor had any player/manager. Kenny did it in his first season. He even scored the goal that won the League Championship.

Proving himself astute in both team selection and on the transfer market he attracted the signatures of Aldridge, Barnes, Beardsley, Houghton, Jamie Redknapp and Steve McMahon amongst others. His vision of a youth policy inspired many of the current crop of youngsters on which Liverpool are building their future.

Before his resignation in February 1991 the club enjoyed further championship and FA Cup success as well as coming within a whisker of another two

*Kenny Dalglish - Considered to be the finest player to have graced Anfield in recent times.
Signed in 1977 from Glasgow Celtic for a record fee of £440,000, Dalglish filled the void left by Keegan's
departure.*

double wins. A sullen and grey looking Dalglish broke the hearts of Liverpool fans across the country as he spelled out the reasons for his decision. Within the year he was back in the game. Taking over the reigns at Blackburn Rovers. He steered the Lancashire club to promotion and the Premiership title within three seasons before taking a job upstairs at Ewood Park. A fairly average spell at Newcastle United prompted him to leave the game once more until his appointment as Glasgow Celtic's technical director. His tenure in that post ended with the selection of Martin O'Neill as team manager in the summer of 2000. Latterly apart from attending Liverpool games as a keen spectator Kenny has worked as a TV pundit but continues to see his name linked with various managerial vacancies.

Paul Dalglish

With a surname like Dalglish he had an awful lot to live up to. He isn't just the son of any old Liverpool player he is Kenny Dalglish's son. He spent a short period at Anfield before following directly in his father's footsteps by signing for Glasgow Celtic. Dalglish Jnr didn't enjoy the same level of success at Parkhead. Progressing no further than the reserves and was given a free after he sought a return to England. No doubt a little homesick he returned to the place he had spent most of his youth at the beginning of the 1996-97 campaign - Anfield.

Again he progressed no further than the second string and despite scoring a huge amount of goals for the 'A' side he was released joining his father at Newcastle United after he had already agreed a loan spell with Bury. He honoured his commitment to the Gigg Lane outfit and made a few first team appearances once he arrived at St James Park. Under Rudd Guillet he was forced out of the picture and signed for Norwich City. The move to Norfolk didn't work out as well as either player and club hoped and a return to the North West for a loan to Wigan Athletic brought a welcome return to first team action.

With the young striker in their side The Latics reached the 2nd Division play-offs but were knocked out at the semi-final stage by Reading. Paul has spent the bulk of his career in the lower leagues.

Defeats

The club's record League defeat came against Birmingham City in Division 2 on 11th December 1954. Billy Liddell scored after 16 minutes in the 9-1 defeat at St Andrews.

Defensive Records

Liverpool's best defensive record over the course of a season came in the 1978-79 campaign. In 42 games a defence crammed with many names which would make any forward line shudder let a paltry 16 goals past them. 12 away from home and a miserly 4 at Anfield. Liverpool won the championship that season which may go some way to proving that a good backline is the cornerstone of a winning team. Certainly Mssrs. Neal, Clemence, Kennedy, Thompson, Hansen and Hughes can claim to have been a huge factor in that triumph. On just one occasion did any team score more than once in a game. Aston Villa beat The Reds 3-1 at Villa Park. That mean spirit was carried over to the cup competitions. In the FA Cup Liverpool conceded their first goal at the semi-final stage when Manchester United fought out a 2-2 draw at Maine Road. The replay at Goodison Park saw The Reds bow out to a Jimmy Greenhoff goal. The League Cup was nothing more than its usual early season distraction to the club. Sheffield United took The Reds' scalps by a single goal victory at Bramall Lane. There was equal disappointment in Europe. Nottingham Forest provided the first hurdle. As the reigning league champions they were always going to be stiff competition - and so it proved. A 2-0 victory at the City Ground was decisive as the second leg at Anfield ended goalless.

In 1990-91 Arsenal powered to the championship conceding just 18 goals over a 38 game campaign. Liverpool had 18 goals recorded against them in winning the 1893-94 Second Division crown. The club were also unbeaten. However, that was over an extremely truncated season comprising just 28 games. Liverpool's next best mark over a 42 game term came on three separate occasions. 24 goals were conceded in the 1968-69, 1970-71 and 1987-88 seasons.

The Derby

Without doubt the most intense and eagerly fought rivalry in club soccer is the Merseyside Derby. The first clash between the city's two teams took place on 13th October 1894 at Goodison Park. Everton took first blood cruising to a 3-0 victory. Anfield staged its first Derby just over a month later. It finished 2-2. Jimmy Ross equalised with a penalty in the dying minutes.

A little known fact is that all league matches between the clubs have taken place in England's top division. Up until the end of the 2002-03 season the Mersey giants had taken each other on 192 times. The breakdown in each competition is as follows:

	P	W	D	L
Football/ Premier League	168	61	53	54
FA Cup	20	9	5	6
League Cup	4	2	1	1
Others	55	29	17	9
(Charity Shield, War time games and Screen Sport Super Cup)				
Total	247	101	76	70

Reds fans have had plenty of opportunity to crow about their superiority but never more so than when enjoying big wins, of which their have been plenty. As early as 1922 a capacity crowd saw Liverpool run out 5-1 home winners. Anfield played host to another six goal encounter 13 years later only this time Liverpool scored them all. Fred Howe proved to be the day's hero bagging four. Legendary marksman and scourge of all Evertonians, Ian Rush, notched the same amount in the devastating 5-0 victory at Goodison Park in November 1982. The Reds' best win away win in Derby history.

In terms of high scoring by both sides the greatest aggregate score in a game came in February 1933. Harold Barton scored a hat-trick in Liverpool's 7-4 home win. The FA Cup fifth round tie between the Mersey giants in 1967 was witnessed by over 100,000 fans of both clubs. 64,851 crammed in to Goodison to watch the home side squeeze through by a single goal. Across Stanley Park 40,149 fans watched events unfold on close circuit television.

The top ten appearance makers in the fixture are as follows:

1	Ian Rush	36
2	Bruce Grobbelaar	33
3	Alan Hansen	32
4	Ian Callaghan	31
5	Phil Neal	29
6	Ronnie Whelan	29
7	Ray Clemence	27
8	Tommy Smith	27
9	Emlyn Hughes	26
10 =	Arthur Goddard	25
	Steve Nicol	25

Disallowed Goals

Billy Liddell scored one of the most talked about goals that never was in the replayed 5th round FA Cup tie with Manchester City at Anfield in February 1956. City led 2-1 with seconds remaining when Liddell gained possession on the halfway line before bursting down the flank. Checking inside he unleashed a fierce shot past Bert Trautmann. The ball had crashed in only for the referee to rule that he had already blown his whistle.

However, for sheer quantity it would be hard to beat the day The Reds had six goals disallowed in the same game. The tally is still a league record and came during the 1-0 defeat by Blackburn Rovers at Ewood Park on 5th September 1896. The game was officiated by a Mr CE Sutcliffe.

Dismissals

The record for the most amount of players sent off in a Football league match involving Liverpool is three. It was set on Valentine's Day 1925 when The Reds played host to Newcastle United. Jock McNab and Walter Wadsworth were sent off for the home side. Tommy Urwin for the visitors. Former Anfield defender Rigobert Song is the only player to have been sent off in the final stages of two World Cups - in 1990 and 1994.

Double Acts

Mention a player's name and more often than not another will spring instantly to mind. Rush and Dalglish are a famous pairing. Gifted individuals in their own right but together they were nothing short of lethal. Ian Rush was a goal scoring thoroughbred. From any angle or distance and with any part of his anatomy he would send an effort goal wards and usually beat the keeper. Dalglish was the perfect foil. His vision, passing and quickness of thought created the space for Rush to exploit. Not that the Scotsman was any slouch in front of goal himself. Kenny weighed in with more than his fair share. The partnership was good for more than 300 strikes.

Forward partnerships have a long and distinguished history at Liverpool. In the modern era Ian St John and Roger Hunt were a major force in the promotion push of the 1960's.

Their goals also propelled The Reds into becoming a big name in the European game. In the seasons and 312 league games they played together 289 goals were scored by at least one of the duo. The Saint was a towering figure with outstanding aerial ability - among other ball skills. Sir Roger as The Kop affectionately dubbed him was without doubt one of the greatest goal scorers of his day and rightly sent shivers down the back of opposition defenders. He was a devastating finisher as his 285 career goals for Liverpool show.

The early part of the next decade saw another fantastic double act occupy The Reds' forward line. In November 1970 John Toshack signed for Liverpool. The Welshman's impact was almost immediate. A goal in a thrilling 3-2 home win over Everton is a start guaranteed to endear any newcomer to Liverpudlian hearts. At the end of that season he had played 21 league games and scored five times. The conclusion of the campaign coincided with the arrival of a diminutive striker from Scunthorpe United. That man was Kevin Keegan who also went some way to repaying his meagre £35,000 fee by scoring on his debut. Almost 51,000 fans saw him open his Anfield account after just 12 minutes. Toshack and Keegan both started the game and the next seven. They didn't set the world alight but there were signs that the partnership could go places. Unfortunately injury and relegation down a pecking order which included players such as Alun Evans, Phil Boersma and Brian Hall frustrated Toshack so much that he almost signed for Leicester City. In fact but for failing a medical he would have left Merseyside for a new start at Filbert Street. It was a blow which could have demoralised a lesser man but it only served to galvanise Tosh's determination. There were further injury lay offs and throughout the six seasons he was paired with Keegan. Toshack rarely made more than 30 league and cup appearances. Despite this the two could be relied upon to supply anything from 20-30 strikes in a season. European and domestic honours rained in as fast as those goals. The pinnacle of the duo's time together also marked its end.

The 1977 European Cup final in Rome was perhaps a fitting way to conclude the partnership. Even though neither got on the scoresheet this match was the end product of all their labours in league and European competition over the years. They could not have made Liverpool the team they were by themselves but without such a deadly striking partnership the club may never have been able to test themselves in such a grand stage.

Players have combined to great effect in other areas of the field. The genealogy of one of the most awesome defensive units in British football can be traced back to the mid 60's. Ron Yeats and Gordon Milne could be described as the epitome of silk and steel. They combined to create a formidable defensive unit with Big Ron using his size and ball winning to great effect. Opponents appeared to be swatted away by the giant centre back. He was almost unbeatable in the air too. For his part Milne was a neat and skilful player with a great eye for goal. The two proved to be the bedrock of Liverpool's push to Division One and the championships won during the latter half of the 60s. The next major partnership charged to make sure none should breach the Liverpool defence came in the shape of Emlyn Hughes and Larry Lloyd. Emlyn was a crowd pleaser who had boundless enthusiasm and a willingness to run himself into the ground if The Reds' cause needed it. Phil Thompson filled the gap Larry's move to Nottingham Forest left. Towards the end of the 1970's Alan Hansen's name began to feature more and more on the team sheet. Initially this was due to injury to either of the regular centre back pairing but eventually the Scot's berth in the first team became a regular one. Until his retirement in 1991 Alan Hansen formed the backbone of a more than dependable Reds defence. Phil Thompson's departure in 1983 was a direct result of what is seen as one of the greatest defensive partnerships of the modern era. Hansen and Lawrenson. Two classy players who combined speed, agility, good tackling and more importantly the ability to anticipate play to some effect.

Swiss international Stephane Henchoz and Fin Sami Hyppia formed an equally formidable pairing as Liverpool's defence became the meanest in the Premiership by the close of the 1999-2000 season. Henchoz had missed a few games during the early part of the season but when the two eventually managed to string a few games together it became clear that Liverpool had something of equal quality to the Lawrenson and Hansen days.

E

Dick Edmed

Without doubt Edmed was one of Liverpool's early great wingers. He started his first season in pole position having relieved Cyril Oxley of his duties. The reason why became very clear. Although he was not in the mould of a Stanley Matthews or Tom Finney he was highly effective at holding his line, beating defenders and sending in passes for others. He was also highly effective when faced with opportunities himself. Notching six in his first season and 14 in the next. In that second season he had assumed the responsibility of taking penalty kicks from Dick Forshaw who had defected to Everton but only two of those 14 goals came from the spot and the following season he scored 16 having left his penalty taking duties to Robert Done.

Injury restricted his number of appearances over the next two campaigns and despite starting the first 12 games of the 1930-31 season he joined Bolton Wanderers. Liverpool had hammered The Trotters 7-2 at Anfield in the fourth game of the season with Edmed scoring two before the break. They clearly saw something they liked and with Harold Barton availing himself of the opportunity he had been given when replacing Edmed, Bolton pounced. The Lancashire club gained some form of revenge for that 7-2 defeat in the final game of the following term beating The Reds 8-1 at Burnden Park despite Liverpool scoring as early as the ninth minute. Edmed rubbed salt in the wound by getting on the scoresheet against his former employers. The injuries that had limited his chances at Anfield caught up with Edmed a few months later forcing him to call time on his illustrious career long before he should have had to. He took a coaching post with Gillingham soon after hanging up his boots staying at Priestfield for some years.

The European Cup

Following promotion in 1962 Liverpool's second season in the top flight not only landed a first championship in 25 years it guaranteed the club's first appearance in the European Champions Cup. The Reds had spent the best part of a decade in Division Two. European competition only began in the early 50's and as a consequence the door had been shut.

On September 14th 1964 The Reds began their adventure in one of Europe's furthest and coldest outposts. KS Reykjavik of Iceland provided the opposition in the preliminary round. They were soundly beaten 5-0 to set up an aggregate 11-1 win for Liverpool.

Nobody could have known or even expected it, but that game set in motion one of the club's most eventful European Cup campaigns. Belgian Champions Anderlecht were next up. They were expected to provided a far sturdier opposition than the Icelandic part-timers but were comprehensively dispatched 4-0 over the two legs. Cologne of West Germany proved a tougher hurdle. The teams played out scoreless draws so had to replay at a neutral venue. Rotterdam hosted their next meeting - a 2-2 draw. No further replay was scheduled and penalties were not used to decide matches at the time.

Progress would be decided by nothing short of luck. A disc, one side white the other red would be tossed. Should it land with the red sector facing up Liverpool would go through to the semi-finals. It did and The Reds went on to meet Inter Milan but only after the disc had ended on its edge on the first throw.

Inter were said to be the world's greatest club side but when faced with the mighty Kop they quivered. Liverpool were basking in the first ever FA Cup glory. Both club and fans had waited so long for the trophy to come to Anfield. Three days after it had finally arrived the ground was understandably buzzing. Shanks, ever the master tactician, decided that the crowd and the atmosphere they had generated could be used to Liverpool's advantage. Injured, but heroic, duo Gerry Byrne and Gordon Milne paraded the cup before the packed stands. The reaction was nothing short of tumultuous. The fans reacted exactly how Bill had wanted them to. They were baying for further glory and set about playing their part in it. Roger Hunt scored in the opening five minutes and although Mazzola equalised there was no stopping the Reds that night. The game finished 3-1 but such was The Reds' superiority the score could so easily have been in double figures. Unfortunately the return leg went as badly as it could have done. Liverpool went down 3-0 amid many allegations of bribery. There was plenty of evidence on which to build a claim.

Liverpool's pursuit of Europe's ultimate prize failed to reach such dizzy heights until the 1976-77 season. Both attempts since that night in the San Siro had ended at the 2nd Round. Ajax gave The Reds an embarrassing lesson in 1966 going through 7-3 on aggregate after a crushing 5-1 win in Holland in the first leg. Red Star Belgrade were more beatable but the Yugoslavs went through after 2-1 wins home and away. Liverpool had lost ground in both games only managing to score through late goals. Three years on and everything had changed. Liverpool were a recognised force on the continent having secured a second UEFA Cup win and eased their way through to the quarter-finals after comfortable wins over Crusaders and Trabzonspur of Turkey. French champions St Etienne were next up and on one of the most memorable nights in the club's history Bob Paisley's men marched on to the last four.

The maths was simple. Liverpool needed to win the 2nd leg at Anfield by two clear goals following a 1-0 defeat across The Channel and when Kevin Keegan levelled the tie with a cross-cum-shot two minutes in to the game a win seemed on the cards. St Etienne restored their advantage with a superb goal from Bathenay just after the break and in the process scored a vital away goal which meant that even Ray Kennedy's strike nine minutes later wouldn't be enough. Just six minutes remained when Kennedy lobbed a speculative ball into the path of David Fairclough who had joined the fray as a substitute for John Toshack, and true to his 'Supersub' tag he managed to edge his way past the covering defenders and in on goal before shooting low and true past the keeper.

Zurich were made light work of in the semi-finals setting up a final with Germany's Borussia Monchengladbach. Liverpool led at the break through Terry McDermott making the most of the space Steve Heighway had bought him from the wing just before the half hour. Danish striker Alan Simonsen fired past Ray Clemence when Jimmy Case played a loose ball in defence a few minutes into the second half but The Reds reclaimed the lead from a most unlikely source when veteran defender Tommy Smith rose above everyone to send a firm header into the net from a corner. A quarter of the game remained but Liverpool refused to take their foot off the gas making the game safe from a Phil Neal penalty eight minutes from the end. A foul on Kevin Keegan who was playing his last match for the club earning the spot-kick.

Twelve months later Liverpool were defending their trophy on home soil with Wembley selected as the venue for the final. Bruges were charged with the job of stopping The Reds and held their lines until a perfectly weighted pass from Graeme Souness set up Kenny Dalglish with a chance. The man bought to fill Keegan's boots lifted a delicate lob over the keeper to set up a comfortable if narrow win. There was none of the drama of the previous year's run as Liverpool eased their way through to face The Belgian champions but momentous occasions came in the shape of a 2-1 win at Benfica's imposing Stadium of Light in the process of which Liverpool ended their opponent's 46 game run without defeat. The previous year's beaten finalists provided a tough challenge in the last four and after a 2-1 defeat in Germany it seemed a reversal of fortune was possible but Liverpool stormed through with a 3-0 win back at Anfield a fortnight after that reverse.

It took Liverpool another three years to reach the final again. Nottingham Forest had snatched Liverpool's crown as English champions but as cup holders The

Reds made another assault on the trophy. Their chances of winning three on the bounce were ended when the two English clubs were drawn together in the 1st round. Brian Clough's side won 2-0 at The City Ground and held on for a goalless draw at Anfield. Eventually going on to wrestle the European Cup from Liverpool's grasp as well. There was some level of compensation as Liverpool regained the domestic championship but while Forest equalled The Reds' feat of regaining the trophy Liverpool were forced to concentrate their efforts on the league once more after falling at the first hurdle again. This time to Dinamo Tbilisi who went through courtesy of a 3-0 home win in the 2nd leg. Making the aggregate score 4-2.

In the 1950s and in terms of Europe, Real Madrid were the greatest achievers having won the first five finals and regained the trophy in 1966. Since that time the Spanish giants had only managed to further their list of domestic honours. They got a chance to regain the trophy in the 1981 final but they were far from the side they had been three decades ago and defended deep in order to keep Liverpool at bay. Despite a few efforts, the Reds were a long way from the side that had won their way to the Parc des Princes courtesy of a 1-1 draw with Bayern Munich after a goalless 1st leg at Anfield. Although through on the away goals rule the victory was well deserved. The script for the second half ran to the same plan so with just under 10 minutes remaining it seemed extra-time was beckoning. However, a Kennedy double act brought the European Cup back to Liverpool for a third time. Ray Kennedy took a throw on the left which fell to the feet of his namesake Alan. The left back edged into the penalty area before unleashing a shot past Agustin.

The same player proved to be the match winner when Liverpool next conquered Europe's finest in 1984. Another major player in that victory was Bruce Grobbelaar the eccentric keeper who had replaced Ray Clemence after that game against Real Madrid. In the two intervening campaigns Grobbelaar had been cast as the villain for two successive exits. Against CSKA Sofia at the quarter-final stage of the 1981-82 competition when Liverpool held a 1-0 lead after the opening tie at Anfield. In the return game slips allowed the Bulgarians to pull off a 2-0 win on the night.

Further Eastern Bloc opposition came at the same stage the following season. Widzew Lodz were a stern test for The Reds boasting one of the most feared forwards in the game in Boniek but Liverpool's chances of going on to the last four were seen as good so long as they brought a decent result back from Poland. Once again Liverpool lost 2-0 with their goalkeeper at least culpable for one of the goals and arguably the second. The Reds won 3-2 at Anfield but despite gaining some respectability in terms of the scoreline Liverpool were still trailing until the last 10 minutes.

The venue for the final was Rome's Olympic Stadium scene of Liverpool's first European Cup glory. Only this time the opposition were the home side - Roma. Phil Neal scored his second goal in European Cup finals after 15 minutes latching on to a loose ball inside the area. The lead could easily have been extended but in the event Pruzzo levelled minutes before half-time. The Reds kept their composure despite the intimidating atmosphere inside the ground continuously probing forward but holding their lines when called to. There were no further goals during the 90 minutes or extra-time forcing the sides to endure a penalty shoot-out. The kicks were taken directly in front of the Roma fans who jeered and whistled as youngster Steve Nicol stepped up to take the first kick. The defender was a willing volunteer but probably wished he hadn't bothered when to the delight of most fans in the stadium he spooned his effort over the bar.

Roma skipper Di Bartolomei coolly dispatched his effort to retain the initiative. Phil Neal, the man usually trusted with penalties, was equally composed. Bruno Contio missed after Bruce Grobbelaar decided to employ a bit of gamesmanship with antics on the line notably biting the net and wobbling his legs in the vital seconds before Conti took his kick. The effort sailed in to the night sky as high as Steve Nicol's had done some minutes earlier. Graeme Souness also converted his chance as did Righetti to make it 2-2. Ian Rush put the pressure on Graziani who two years earlier had won the World Cup with Italy by sliding his effort home. Grobbelaar repeated his routine for the new opponent who also shot high and wide. The next red shirt to step forward belonged to Alan Kennedy the man whose goal had won the cup three years earlier. He hit a shot firmly to his left sending the keeper the wrong way to secure a win against all the odds.

Liverpool reached one more final coming up against Juventus the following season at the Heysel Stadium in Brussels. The events leading up to the game made the result meaningless. Although the record books will show Juventus won by a single goal - a penalty 90 seconds in to the game - the death of 39 fans before the game after a wall collapsed during rioting between the opposing fans superseded any thoughts of victory. That incident along with numerous others at which English fans were deemed to be the instigators led to English clubs being banned from European competition indefinitely. The ban was lifted for all clubs except Liverpool in 1990 who were allowed to rejoin two years later.

The Reds recorded their last championship in 1990 and had not finished in a high enough league position since the goalposts of eligibility were widened until 2001. Although teams no longer need to be national champions in order to qualify for Europe's elite club tournament Liverpool made a welcome return to the competition they dominated during the late 1970s and early 1980s by virtue of a third place finish to the 2000-01 season. Although it marked The Reds' first appearance at the preliminary stage since 1965 a mirror on the past achievements could be seen in the fact that Liverpool lifted the European Cup for the first time on the back of a UEFA Cup triumph achieved in a tense finish.

However, despite looking a decent bet to progress to the last four after negotiating the two group stages defeat by Bayer Laverkusen saw the German side clash with Manchester United in the semi-final. As Premiership runners-up 12 months later Liverpool bypassed the qualifying rounds but poor results saw The Reds crash out at the first hurdle.

European Super Cup

In November 1977 Liverpool, as European Cup holders, took on Kevin Keegan's new side SV Hamburg - the European Cup Winners' Cup holders. A closely fought 1-1 draw in Germany was followed by a 6-0 hammering at Anfield as Liverpool cruised to a stylish 7-1 aggregate victory. Just over a year later Anderlecht contested The Reds for the right to call themselves Europe's super club.

The Belgian side took the honours after a 3-1 home win and a 2-1 defeat at Anfield made it 4-3 in their favour over the two legs. The trophy was decided by a single game in 1985. Juventus were hosts and made that home advantage pay with a comfortable 2-0 win. As UEFA Cup holders Liverpool contested the trophy with European Cup holders Bayern Munich a few weeks into the 2001-02 season. A 3-2 win allowed The Reds to claim a fifth piece of silverware in a little over six months. John Arne Riisse, Michael Owen and Emile Heskey's goals were enough to ensure Liverpool won the game despite a spirited fight back from Bayern.

Alun Evans

This gifted but ultimately flawed young player could go down as one of soccer's greatest enigmas. He came to Anfield in a blaze of hype - mostly due to the £100,000 fee Bill Shankly thought the teenager was worth. The transfer followed hard on the heels of a list of fine displays for Wolves. Opposition defences were torn to shreds. That was in September 1968 but as the new decade got into full stride Alun Evan's Liverpool career was coming to a juddering halt. The promise that had seen him marked down as one of the game's brightest stars had deserted him. Despite turning out in every remaining first team game that season a return of seven goals from 33 games was disappointing.

Liverpool had a glut of quality forward players and this along with a severe cartilage injury restricted him to around 50 appearances over the next three seasons. A nightclub incident which left a highly visible scar on his right cheek may also have taken its toll on a young man with so much resting on his shoulders. When he left for Aston Villa in 1972 the fee was £70,000. Moves to Walsall and Australian outfit Hellas, took up the remainder of his professional career.

His Anfield stay wasn't all doom and gloom. 1970-71 proved his most consistent season for The Reds. He started the first 11 games scoring six goals in the process. Injury took him out of the side until March but that initial goal ratio was more or less maintained. The Reds were eventually knocked out of the European Fairs Cup courtesy of a home defeat by Leeds United at the semi-final stage but the previous round had paired Liverpool with the mighty Bayern Munich. Alun Evans gave the great Franz Beckenbauer the chasing of his life. The Kaiser left Anfield with a very battered pride following Evans' hat-trick.

Roy Evans

When Roy Evans retired from professional football at the tender age of 25 nobody could have predicted just how a man with 11 first team run outs would prove such an integral force in one club's monopolisation of the European and domestic game. Shanks may not have thought he would make the top grade as a player but he seemed to have very little doubt in his abilities as a coach. The youngest member of the bootroom was given the task of managing the reserves. His first three years in the job reaped a hat-trick of Central League titles. A slight blip followed as the subsequent season saw The Reds' second string finish as runners up. The next four campaigns saw the championship stay at Anfield and while an unusual dip in fortunes hit in 1982-83 as the team finished 6th the last two years of Roy's stewardship brought even more reserve glory.

Eight Central League titles in a decade had some marking him down as a future first team manager. He had admirers at every level not least in the boardroom.

When Joe Fagan retired after the Heysel Stadium disaster in 1985 there seemed every possibility of the amiable Roy Evans stepping into the job. In the end there was a change of role for him but it wasn't for the big chair. He became a first team coach as Phil Thompson returned to the club to take the helm with the reserves. Quietly and methodically Evans displayed the professional veneer his bootroom apprenticeship had bestowed upon him. Questions about his managerial ambitions continued to be put but as far as Roy was concerned the job he held was the only one he wanted. He was a just a cog in the wheels which ensured Liverpool stayed one step ahead of the rest.

No doubt Graeme Souness, like Kenny Dalglish before him, relied on the advice of over 20 years intricate knowledge of Liverpool FC. Eventually the man who had for so long seemed likely to be king came to the throne when Souness resigned in January 1995. He had been officially designated as the Scot's assistant following a tumultuous end to the previous season.

Hot on the heels of a couple of very difficult seasons the move was met with a wave of optimism. Hope was fulfilled with a League Cup win during the new man's first full season in charge. Challenges for the Premiership crown also promised much but as the final leg of the championship race unfurled before them the Reds only succeeded in taking faltering steps towards the finishing line when nothing short of strident gallops were required.

There seemed a chance of FA Cup glory in 1996. Liverpool had made very impressive noises in their progress to Wembley but succumbed to a single goal just minutes before time in a very disappointing display against Manchester United. First is everything at Anfield and unfortunately Roy's frustrating search for pole position had some questioning whether he was the right man for the post. Those who argued against him saw their cause bolstered when name after name was linked with the Liverpool manager's job. Just as many alternative roles were mooted for Evans. The appointment of Gerard Houllier as joint manager following France's World Cup triumph in the summer of 1998 was seen as a sign that the Anfield board were running out of patience and wanted to change things round in order to bring that much craved success.

As technical director of the world champions Houllier's services were highly sought. Not just in the UK but all over Europe - but a personal affinity with the club and many long friendships with members of the Anfield hierarchy saw him return to Merseyside where he taught in the 1960's.

Whether two men could share the responsibility caused much debate. Who would have the final say over team selection, training methods, or discipline? The overwhelming majority seemed to think that it couldn't work and so it proved. A poor run of results culminating in defeat to Derby County in November 1998 finally brought the curtain down on the career of one of Anfield's most devoted sons.

Ever Presents

The record number of ever presents in a league season is five. This has happened in three separate seasons. Gerry Byrne, Ian Callaghan, Tommy Lawrence, Tommy Smith and Ron Yeats featured in every game of the 1965-66 campaign. Of these five only Gerry Byrne missed so much as one of the 15 cup ties also played that term. In 1968-69 Tommy Lawrence, Chris Lawler, Tommy Smith, Ian Callaghan and Peter Thompson were the only players to make it on to every team sheet. All bar Tommy Lawrence made it through the nine cup games.

The last squad to equal that record was the 1983-84 championship winners. Bruce Grobbelaar, Alan Kennedy, Mark Lawrenson, Alan Hansen and Sammy Lee certainly played their part in that glory and the capture of an historic, if strength sapping, league, European and League Cup treble which added another 24 games to the programme. Of these only Mark Lawrenson missed out on completing all 66 games.

The individual accolade for the most amount of ever present seasons during their Liverpool career belongs to Phil Neal. Of his eleven and a half seasons with the club nine were 100% fulfilled.

Amazingly eight of these campaigns came in successive seasons from 1975-76 to 1982-83.

F

The FA Cup

Until The Reds secured a first FA Cup final win in 1965 it had been a case of so near yet so far. Due to this bad fortune it was said that if the club ever did win the trophy the Liver Birds would fly off their famous dockside perches. The Cup was 21 years old before Liverpool's competition debut in 1892. Nantwich provided the opposition in the first qualifying round. A 4-0 victory set up a tie with Newton Heath (now more commonly known as Manchester United) in the second round of qualification. It marked Anfield's first opportunity to host cup visitors and a bumper 40,000 crowd witnessed the 9-0 trouncing. It proved a short lived campaign as Cheshire based Northwich Victoria won through the next round.

In 1895 Liverpool had to beat Barnsley St. Peter's twice in order to reach the second round. The first tie in Yorkshire finished 1-1 after 90 minutes. Liverpool thought they had booked a passage to the next stage following Jimmy Ross' extra-time winner but the Barnsley officials objected on the grounds that extra-time could only be played if both clubs agreed to it. They hadn't and an Anfield replay was ordered. Back on Merseyside Liverpool secured a convincing 4-0 win.

Liverpool reached the cup final for the first time in 1914. Crystal Palace was the venue with the mighty Burnley providing the opposition. It marked the first visit of a reigning monarch to the cup final. King George saw The Reds dominate affairs but ultimately lose by a single goal. The Clarets' defence was under siege for most of the game and things could have been different had Tom Miller's goal not have been disallowed for offside. 36 years later The Reds made their second cup final and their first at Wembley. Everton had been dispatched in the semi-finals setting the scene for a famous victory. Unfortunately there was further heartache when Arsenal ran out 2-0 winners on a day Liverpool did very little to distinguish themselves.

In 1965 it proved a case of third time lucky. Leeds United held The Reds to a scoreless draw over 90 minutes. Roger Hunt scored in extra-time only for Billy Bremner to pull the sides level soon afterwards. Liverpool were far more positive in attack than the Yorkshire side and Ian St John's close range header decided the tie. Following that win fortune still proved a fickle mistress. The latter stages of the competition remained elusive until 1971 when in a repeat of the 1950 final Liverpool took on Arsenal. Having clinched the league title The Gunners were looking to achieve the double. It was a tight game. With both sides difficult to break down it came as no surprise that an extra 30 minutes were needed. When Steve Heighway went on a run before cracking a low drive past Bob Wilson there were high hopes of The Reds holding on to the advantage. George Graham and Charlie George shattered the dream.

After two successive fourth round exits Liverpool pitched up in the final once more. A high flying Newcastle United were well fancied to deny The Reds glory and Malcolm McDonald, the Magpie's centre forward, was only too keen to let everyone know. But as the Liverpool players supped champagne in celebration of a great performance "Super Mac" was forced to eat a post match meal of humble pie while reflecting on the fact that the invincible side he said would prevail were hammered 3-0 in the most one sided cup final for many a year.

Liverpool toyed with Newcastle who in the end just weren't good enough. Everyone connected with the club was ecstatic. Although one Scouser traipsed off the Wembley turf a broken man. Terry McDermott had been missed by the Anfield scouting system but eventually got his chance to make the big time at St James Park. He'd impressed Bob Paisley and by the time the manager had taken charge of his first cup final side three seasons later McDermott was an integral part of the club's midfield. However, for a second time he ended up with a loser's medal as Liverpool lost 2-1 to Manchester United.

Nine years later another of Liverpool's greatest rivals provided the Wembley opposition in the first ever all Merseyside FA Cup Final. It proved a defining moment as for the first time in their illustrious history Liverpool achieved the league and cup double. Ian Rush was the man of the moment with two vital goals in a 3-1 victory. The Welshman was just as instrumental when the teams met again in 1989. Although the final was played in the shadow of the Hillsborough Disaster the win was no less important. John Aldridge put The Reds ahead in the opening minutes only to see Stuart McCall equalise with a scrambled effort in the final seconds. In extra time Rush who had come on as a substitute nosed Liverpool in to the lead only for McCall to equalise once more. However, the club's best ever goalscorer had the last word with a deft header to make it 3-2.

Rush scored his fifth cup final goal (a club and competition record) in 1992 to seal a 2-1 win over Second Division Sunderland. The Reds' run of wins at Wembley was brought to an end in disappointing circumstances when Manchester United beat a very under par Liverpool side with a goal four minutes from time in 1996.

In one of the most pulsating cup finals in many years Liverpool faced Arsenal at The Millennium Stadium in 2001. On a balmy sunny afternoon The Reds playing in their change strip of gold and blue completed a cup double courtesy of late strikes from Michael Owen. The striker had enjoyed something of a mixed season but by the end of the domestic campaign was in fine form having scored five in the two games running up to the final. Swedish international Freddy Ljungberg had put The Gunners ahead with just 15 minutes remaining but Owen brought his tally for the week to seven stabbing home a loose ball in the area seven minutes from time. Five minutes after that he latched on to a Patrik Berger pass before using his pace to edge past Lee Dixon and Tony Adams and fire low past David Seaman from the angle.

Ian Callaghan holds the appearance record in the competition with 88 as a Liverpool player. Liverpool's five FA Cup triumphs came from 11 final appearances. The club have featured at the semi-final stage on 20 occasions.

Other points of note in Liverpool's FA Cup history are that they became the first club to be drawn away from home in all rounds of the competition in 1987-88. The club's highest scorer in the competition is Ian Rush. The Welsh Wizard's total in the cup is 43 for all clubs. Of those strikes 34 came in a Liverpool jersey. Although not a giant killing act The Reds' worst FA Cup defeat was nonetheless embarrassing. Bolton Wanderers hammered five without reply at Burnden Park in January 1946. This was the only season ties were decided over two legs. Four days later Liverpool took the home match 2-0.

The 2001 victory over Arsenal was the first time Liverpool had managed to win the FA Cup in their "away strip". The Gunners were forced to change when the two met in 1971. 21 years earlier Liverpool wore white shirts and black shorts Arsenal sported gold jerseys and white shorts. In 1977 The Reds were forced to wear the same combination against Manchester United and lost. When the two giants of the English game met in the final a quarter of a century later United again won the right to play in their first kit. Liverpool in their white and green quarters lost out once more.

Joe Fagan

Continuing the line of bootroom succession which started with Bill Shankly the popular Liverpool coach was promoted to team manager following Bob Paisley's abdication.

Liverpool born and bred, Fagan's playing days were centred around various other parts of the North West and Yorkshire. Most notably at the other end of The East Lancs Road with Manchester City. Bradford Park Avenue were his only other football league club. The rest of his career was spent in the non-league structure. When his playing days were over Harry Catterick persuaded the recently retired Fagan to become his trainer at Rochdale. He took a similar post at Anfield in 1958. Shank's appointment a year later didn't change his role as he carried on doing the same job day in day out until his elevation to the manager's office in 1983.

At the age of 62 he was generally seen as a short term appointment. So it proved. After just two seasons he decided to call it a day and retire. 28 years at Anfield culminated in the unfortunate scenes at The Heysel Stadium but that couldn't take away the unprecedented glory of a first season in which he led the club to an historic treble of League, League Cup and European Champions Cup. That title win also sealed a hat-trick of championships. A feat only Huddersfield Town and Arsenal had ever achieved. His death after a short illness in July 2001 aged 80 was mourned across Merseyside and beyond.

Willie Fagan

A two season stay at Preston North End was sandwiched between lengthier stays at Glasgow Celtic and Liverpool. The Deepdale club were a force in the English game but having reached the 1937 cup final Fagan decided his future lay elsewhere and signed for Liverpool in October of the same year. He made his debut not long after and managed to score in three consecutive games after that bow against Leicester City. He remained in the side until the season closed scoring nine times in the league and cup. The following term he ended as the club's joint top scorer. His ability to switch from inside forward to a more central role during any stage of the game was responsible for some of this impressive tally.

The battle against Hitler snatched seven seasons away from him although he continued to turn out for the club in war-time games. Injury robbed him of a prolonged run once the Football League reconvened. This was a terrible blow considering he had just been awarded the club captaincy. There was some reward when he helped Liverpool lift the first post-war championship scoring seven goals from the 18 games played. He continued to struggle with fitness over the following two seasons and had to fight to get himself back in the first team picture, but the flame haired Scot showed he had enough fire in his belly to persevere and played 35 times during the 1949-50 season grabbing 11 goals. He was reduced to a bit part player once more making just seven more outings from the end of that season before crossing the Irish Sea to play for Belfast Distillery. It was a short-lived experience ending when the chance to become player/manager of Weymouth beckoned.

David Fairclough

As a boy the striker used to stand on The Kop and cheer his heroes on in some of their greatest moments but the assembled masses on that terrace ended up singing his praises on one of the greatest nights ever at Anfield. He made his debut in November 1975 against Middlesbrough and very quickly earned the tag 'Super Sub' courtesy of his reputation for coming off the bench and scoring vital goals. None will be remembered longer or more fondly than his match winning strike against St Etienne. It was the quarter final stage of the 1977 European Cup. Liverpool went into the 2nd leg trailing by a single goal. All looked well when Kevin Keegan tied the aggregate scores within minutes of the start. The Reds pushed for more but found themselves pegged back after Bathenay struck for the French champions. This meant that Liverpool had to score another two as St Etienne would go through on the away goals rule.

David Fairclough - A striker who earned the tag Supersub for match winning performances after coming off the bench. Fairclough had to battle with the likes of Kenny Dalglish, David Johnson, Kevin Keegan and John Toshack among others for a place in the starting XI.

Consequently, Ray Kennedy's strike minutes later wouldn't be enough to secure passage to the next stage.

When John Toshack limped off the pitch after 77 minutes of combat, head bowed and looking rueful, he knew time was running out. David replaced him and took his place in history. Only six minutes remained when Fairclough made a run which was spotted by Ray Kennedy. His lofted pass fell neatly into the forward's stride, he took a touch on his chest to bring the ball down and away from a St. Etienne defender and in to a one-on-one with Curkovic who advanced to narrow the angle. The ginger haired striker kept his nerve and slid the ball home for victory.

Of the 149 appearances he made 62 were as a substitute. He left Anfield early in 1981 to spend a season in the North American Soccer League but returned to make a further 11 outings - for eight of these he was a substitute. He even finished his final game for the club in the Number 12 shirt. Switzerland and Lucerne was his next port of call. Then it was on to Norwich and Oldham. He saw out his days with Beueren of Belgium.

Family Ties

Footballing skills tend to run in families. Large dynasties of professionals can trace family trees back over many generations. Many do not play for the same team and certainly Liverpool haven't seen a large number. Especially father and son combinations. There are Kenny and Paul Dalglish of course but Dalglish junior never made The Reds' starting eleven. Nor did another Anfield stalwart's offspring, Ashley Neal, son of Phil was a regular in the reserves during the early part of the 90s but never got as far as the first eleven. A duo who buck the trend are Ray Saunders and his son Dean. Between 1952 and 1959 Ray put in 144 first team appearances for The Reds. Dean's career was a little shorter but very eventful. He arrived in 1992 for a domestic transfer record fee of £2.9 million. He left a few years later for Aston Villa.

A few Liverpool players share the surname Jones but only two are related. Bill Jones and his Grandson Rob. Bill joined the club following the war and in his eight seasons at Liverpool made nearly 300 appearances scoring 17 goals in the process. Rob's Anfield career lasted a similar amount of time but reaped no goals whatsoever despite well over 200 first team run outs for the club. Graeme Souness signed the promising young right back from Crewe Alexandra in September 1991. Just days after his arrival on Merseyside he was pitched into a league game at Old Trafford. He acquitted himself well and made his England debut a few months later. A list of injuries and managers' preferences for others limited his first team opportunities and lead to his eventual departure from Anfield in the summer of 1999 as a free agent.

Three sets of brothers have played in the same sides. Hugh and Matt McQueen joined the club from Leith Athletic in time for Liverpool's first Football League campaign. Both proved to be huge successes on Merseyside. Matt played in numerous positions, including goalkeeper, and managed the club once his playing days were over. Hugh's two season stay saw him score 14 goals in his 44 appearances.

Archie and Bill Goldie were teammates for a few years towards the end of the 1800's. Until Archie left the club in 1900 both missed just a handful of games in the three seasons they played together. Tom Miller enjoyed a four year spell at Anfield prior to the First World War but was involved in the match fixing scandal which rocked the footballing world. He was suspended from the game for his part in the deal which ensured Manchester United secured a 2-0 win in April 1915. He came back to the club to play alongside his brother John before departing for Old Trafford in 1920. Walter and Harold Wadsworth were both part of the 1921-22 and 1922-23 league title winning squads but only Walter, or 'Big Waddy' as he was also known, won championship medals. The two played together just over 50 times.

Alex and Dave Watson are the only siblings to have appeared on the books in recent years. Despite having obvious promise Dave was sold to Norwich City in 1980 without having made a single first team appearance for Liverpool. A string of impressive displays over his seasons at Carrow Road earned him a big money return to Merseyside only this time it was for Everton. The Goodison Park faithful continue to hold the former Red in high esteem. Younger brother Alex, also a defender, suffered from the same trouble as Dave - breaking into one of the most established and complete backlines in the league. A handful of run outs were all he could muster so when the chance of regular games with Bournemouth came his way he accepted a move to Dean Court.

Firsts

Liverpool's on field achievements have secured many notable firsts but maybe due to The Reds' knack of being in the right place at the right time there have been a number of off field firsts too. Some quite obscure. For instance linesmen wore fluorescent jerseys for the first time in a league match at Anfield in a game against Derby County on January 20th 1973. Another first for officials at Anfield came on 1st May 1999 when referee Steven Lodge wore an earpiece which allowed him to communicate with his assistants. Liverpool took on Tottenham Hotspur and the trial technology proved vital in the decision to send off Spurs' midfielder Tarrico for a second bookable offence. The Reds finished 3-2 winners after trailing 2-0 at half time.

Liverpool became the first team to win a domestic cup outside England when claiming the Worthington Cup at Cardiff's Millennium Stadium. Gerard Houllier's side returned to the principality three months later to become the first side to win the FA Cup outside England.

Floodlights

Liverpool installed floodlights on October 30th 1957 at a cost of £12,000. They were officially switched on for the first time by the then club Chairman, Mr. T.V. Williams. A specially arranged Derby match was played to mark the occasion. Liverpool won 3-2. Three weeks earlier the teams had met at Goodison Park to celebrate the installation of Everton's floodlighting system. The initial pylon lights at Anfield were replaced by halcyon bulbs attached to the stands in the 1970's.

Football Writers' Player of The Year Award

Ian Callaghan was the first Liverpool player to claim this personal accolade in recognition for his achievements during the 1973-74 season. Kevin Keegan was the next Anfield recipient two years later. Emlyn Hughes made sure the trophy stayed on a Merseyside display cabinet at the end of the following season. Kenny Dalglish capped his second year in English football when he was voted the Football League's best player in 1979. Terry McDermott won it 12 months later. Dalglish became the first Liverpool man to win it twice in 1983, and Ian Rush took the plaudits for his superb goalscoring over the following season. Reds' players retained the trophy for three successive seasons from 1987-88 to 1989-90 as John Barnes, Steve Nicol and then John Barnes again were voted the best in the business by the pundits and those in the press box.

Robbie Fowler

Despite showing immense enthusiasm to the Liverpool cause Robbie Fowler was a devout Evertonian during his youth. It was just The Reds' good fortune that they rather than the team from the other side of Stanley Park managed to spot him first. He began to display the prodigious talent and flair for goal scoring almost as soon as he arrived at the club. The product of Kenny Dalglish's belief in youth policy was given his first run out and repaid the faith shown in him by scoring on his debut - a League Cup tie at Fulham. Liverpool won 3-1. He followed that by scoring all five in the return leg and thereby equalling the record for goals scored in a match by a Liverpool player. In the next League game he scored against Oldham. A few weeks later he scored his first Liverpool hat-trick in a home match with Southampton. Injuries and suspensions apart he virtually remained a first choice striker until the turn of the century.

His partnership with Ian Rush blossomed and the young man freely admitted that most of his development was down to the things the Welshman taught him. Not that he seemed to need much schooling. He beat Rush's record for scoring 100 career goals for The Reds by a single game managing the feat in 165 matches. Typically the century came during a flurry of strikes when Liverpool beat Middlesbrough 5-1. Fowler notched four of them the second of which was the history maker.

In the first game of the 1994-95 campaign he single-handedly finished Arsenal off by notching a hat-trick in just four minutes and 33 seconds. A record which still stands as the fastest in Premiership history. Record signing Stan Collymore took his place for the start of the next season but once an injury to the £8.5million man knocked him out of contention Fowler was back and with a vengeance. Bolton were rocked by the four he put past them and Arsenal were on the receiving end once more as he hit them with another treble. Ian Rush was the man to make way when Collymore returned and by the season's end the pair had 55 goals between them. Robbie Fowler having claimed 36. Alongside Michael Owen and with a contract which would have seen him stay at Anfield well into the next millennium there seemed little doubt that Liverpool would have a very potent attacking force for many years to come. However, the rotation system used by Gerard Houllier was rumoured to have left the striker uneasy. Whatever the truth in the speculation bandied around Robbie was a key member of the Liverpool side which completed the cup treble in 2001 even if he found himself relegated to the bench for the FA and UEFA Cup finals. However, with just a few months of the 2001-2002 season having elapsed he joined Leeds for £11 million.

Friendlies

A club like Liverpool will be invited to take part in a number of high profile friendlies and tours. Matches involving the club have taken part on every continent but some of the more interesting games have involved unusual sides. The Irish Olympic XI used The Reds as a practice opponent on August 19th 1987 in Dublin. Liverpool were 5-0 winners.

Other national teams Liverpool have played against include Saudi Arabia in October 1978 when a 1-1 draw was fought out in Jeddah. South African, Great Britain and England XIs have all provided competition at various stages. High scoring encounters include an 8-7 win over a Bury Select XI on 19th May 1982 and a 9-9 draw against a Bobby Charlton XI on 27th May 1977 in Tommy Smith's testimonial held just two days after Liverpool won the European Cup for the first time. The Anfield Iron's service record will have attracted a large number wishing to pay their goodwill but the presence of the trophy guaranteed a full house.

G

Gary Gillespie

The introduction of a new centre-back when Liverpool already had Mark Lawrenson and Alan Hansen in tandem seemed one of the club's strangest transfer deals of recent times. However, those raising eyebrows were reckoning without the tactical acumen of Joe Fagan who, far from seeking to add another good player to his impressive list of reserves was building for the future and investing in a quality defender. Clearly chances were always going to arise through injury or other reasons and when they did rather than leave a replacement to chance the manager wanted a tried and tested alternative capable of holding the backline as tightly as the man he had replaced.

Opportunities were few and far between for a while so the man who had converted from midfield to defence while at Coventry City had to bide his time. He spent his first full season at the club in the Central League and most of the subsequent term playing second fiddle when, despite covering for Lawrenson in the FA Cup semi-final and scoring a hat-trick in the final home game of the season against Birmingham City, he was forced to give way for the show piece occasion at Wembley thanks to a virus. The cup held no luck for the player who was a loser in 1988 against Wimbledon and lost out through injury 12 months later when The Reds beat Everton.

Versatility across the back four was another reason why the £325,000 capture appealed to the canny Joe Fagan. He was replaced by Kenny Dalglish who was equally astute in his deployment of Gillespie. The departure of Alan Kennedy and absence of Jim Beglin allowed him to slot comfortably in the left back position. He was deployed in other roles including his old haunt in the centre of the park. Barry Venison's arrival on the scene saw him become first choice full-back but with Mark Lawrenson beset by injuries he was forced to retire during the 1987-88 season. Alan Hansen had a tailor made partner as The Reds rewrote the record books during that season and claimed the title at a cantor with five games remaining.

During the next couple of seasons Gillespie was also hit by injury which limited his number of appearances although he did manage to help The Reds clinch the title in 1990 contributing 11 starts and two substitute appearances to the campaign. Graeme Souness had other plans for his defence and by the opening of the new season in August 1991 he had joined Celtic in a £1 million deal. Three seasons later he returned to Highfield Road but played just three times before retiring. Recently he worked as a scout with Portsmouth working under former Anfield teammate John Wark.

Goalkeepers

The list of great Liverpool goalkeepers reads like a Who's Who of the art. It is without doubt a highly specialised position and also one which enjoys a special place in the rich history of the club and usually in the hearts of fans. Many of The Reds' custodians will have already earned their own entry into this book by virtue of their exploits between the sticks. Men such as Harry Storer, Ken Campbell, Elisha Scott, Arthur Riley and Cyril Sidlow are just some of the names from the early part of the century. These legends have been joined by Tommy Younger, Bert Slater, Jimmy Furnell, Tommy Lawrence, Ray Clemence, Bruce Grobbelaar and David James who have stood firm as The Reds' last line of defence. Little wonder the club's telegraph address was GOALKEEPER.

Arthur Goddard

For many years Arthur Goddard held Liverpool's appearance record becoming the first player to turn out in over 400 first team games. The 13 seasons it took him to amass that total were among the most eventful in the early part of Liverpool's history. That he missed so few games over this period especially from the wing - such a high contact area of the field - is testament to both his fitness and sheer strength. The Reds slipped from the top flight but made their way back at the first attempt with Goddard playing 28 games. The following season after contributing 38 appearances Liverpool won the League title. He remained a first choice until the middle of the 1913-14 campaign and the advent of Jackie Sheldon as a contender for his position. In the face of such competition he opted to join Cardiff City the consequence being that he missed out on the chance to appear in Liverpool's first FA Cup final team. Just before he left the club a benefit match was held in respect of his service. £250 was raised.

The Golden Goal

Only once has a game involving The Reds gone into the golden goal extra-time - the UEFA Cup final with Deportivo Alaves. The tie was settled during the 30 minutes when defender Adelfi Geli flicked a header past his own keeper from Gary McAllister's free-kick to make the score 5-4.

Archie Goldie

Scotland has yielded many great players for The Reds over the past hundred years. Knowing that Liverpool needed to inject new blood if they were to reverse the relegation suffered at the close of the 1894-95 season a scouting mission was launched. One of the faces introduced was Clyde's Archie Goldie. A full-back who brought some much needed stability to the defence. This was perhaps best illustrated by the fact that Liverpool could fall prey to needless and sometimes heavy defeats in his absence. Fortunately he didn't miss too many games over his five seasons at Anfield.

However, although his powers of recovery after injury were swift he suffered a severe set back during the opening months of the season forcing him to miss 13 matches. The most he had ever had to sit out. Although he played in the last 18 games of the campaign that season was his last with Liverpool. He moved on during the summer missing out on the club's first league championship the following term. A tough defender with an equally robust tackle he was a formidable opponent who never knew when he or his club was beaten. A spirit best typified by the game in which he scored his one and only goal for the club. That came in a 4-3 defeat at Sunderland's Roker Park. Liverpool trailed 3-0 at half-time and with 18 minutes to go Archie Goldie's strike off his trusty right boot gave The Reds a little respectability if nothing else, but when that strike was followed by efforts from Malcolm McVean and George Allan within the last five minutes it seemed Liverpool had pulled an unlikely result out of the bag. Within two seasons of joining The Reds Archie was joined at the club by his brother Bill.

Bill Goldie

Procured from the same source as his elder sibling Archie Bill Goldie arrived from Clyde where he also played as a full-back, but a switch to the wing-half position proved to be a new lease of life for the player who would undoubtedly have struggled to oust his brother from the team. Both Archie and Bill were good players in their own right though very different and were comfortably accommodated in the same team for just over two seasons. Whilst Archie was a well disciplined defender who did his job in a methodical if unspectacular fashion Bill showed he was a player who possessed flair as well as technique and for many seasons including that title winning campaign of 1900-01 Liverpool's goalscoring record was second to none. In no small part this was due to the cutting passes supplied and runs made by Bill Goldie.

He left Liverpool in 1903 to join Fulham after three seasons as an ever present had pushed his appearance record well over 150 in the league alone. From Craven Cottage he finished his career with Leicester Fosse still displaying the same form that had helped lift Liverpool to the pinnacle of the domestic game.

Bobby Graham

As a tender 19 year old debutante fresh from finishing his apprenticeship the Motherwell born striker scored a hat-trick against Aston Villa. Liverpool won the game 5-1. He had been covering for fellow Scot Gordon Wallace who had suffered an injury which would keep him out for most of the season. After a start like that and with a first team regular sidelined it seemed all was set for Bobby Graham to enjoy an extended run and stake a claim to become yet another in a long list of legendary Liverpool strikers. He scored the final goal in the next game a 3-1 win over Sheffield United but fired blanks for the other 12 games he played although he did manage to score in the 6-1 demolition of Icelandic part-timers KR Reykjavik in the European Cup.

Injury caught up with the youngster who found games and consequently goals hard to come by over the next four seasons. His best return being five from the 11 starts and one substitute appearance he made during the 1968-69 season. This was still a useful average and the following campaign with Alan Evans injured plus Ian St John and Roger Hunt also missing games and finding their old touches hard to regain Graham managed to figure in every game Liverpool played - 54 in total across four competitions. Bobby had matured as a player and looked the genuine article as a long term successor to Hunt, St John and all those great strikers that had gone before him over the past decade. However, just 10 games into the next season he broke his ankle against Chelsea and was laid up for the best part of four months managing just four sporadic starts and a a substitute appearance.

During this enforced lay off John Toshack signed for the club. In the close season before the 1971-72 campaign Kevin Keegan was also drafted in leaving Bobby with no option but to seek a move if he was to play first team football. Coventry City bid £70,000 for his services, a considerable chunk of the combined prices paid for Toshack and Keegan and a sound piece of transfer economics. After two seasons at Highfield Road he returned to Merseyside for a loan spell with Tranmere Rovers. A permanent home for his talents was next found in his home town of Motherwell where he remained for four years before spending a similar amount of time with Hamilton Academicals.

Bruce Grobbelaar

A man for whom the word 'crowd favourite' was invented. Home or away Bruce Grobbelaar always pleased his public. Although famed for his clowning he was just as notorious for the great saves he made. They should never be forgotten as they were both countless and invariably match winners or at the very least point savers. The leap to tip Graham Sharpe's header over the bar in the 1986 FA Cup Final and the spaghetti legs during the penalty shoot out which decided the 1984 European Cup final may spring instantly to mind but week in, week out, no matter what the competition or stage of the season the South African born 'No.1' was rarely found wanting. You do not spend 13 seasons at Anfield - including five as a consecutive ever-present without giving your all nor without having a considerable amount to offer.

Bruce's route into top flight football, as suits his character was unusual. Following active service in the army he joined Vancouver Whitecaps in the late 70's. He spent the latter part of the 1979-80 season with Crewe Alexandra and actually scored a penalty in his last game for the club. He returned to Canada and remained in the North American Soccer League until Liverpool signed him in March 1981. A £250,000 bid was accepted and although initially said to be a long term replacement for Ray Clemence. Clem's move to Spurs a few months later thrust him straight into the spotlight.

Despite a rocky start the management persevered and until his eventual departure in 1995 he served the club with distinction in over 500 games seeing off competition from Bob Boulder, Mike Hooper and gave David James a good run for his money before the younger man finally ousted him from between the sticks.

H

Brian Hall

The Liverpool University student was an amateur player at Anfield before he was invited to report with the first team squad for pre-season training. He arrived at Melwood in his bus conductor's uniform as he was working during his summer vacation. This prompted Bill Shankly to ask whether you needed a degree to work on public transport. He went on to pass his studies and became known as 'Little Bamber' in the dressing room. He spent eight years on Merseyside before leaving for Plymouth Argyle. When his playing career finished he became a school teacher in his native Preston. He returned to Anfield in the summer of 1991 to take on the community liaison and public relations brief at the club.

Alf Hanson

Local product Alf Hanson was one of the men behind the prolific goalscoring record maintained by Gordon Hodgson. The Bootle born winger supplied many pinpoint crosses from the left. The accuracy of his passes was matched by the blinding pace and control which took him past so many opposition defenders. As well as supplying the ammunition he also fired more than his fair share scoring 52 goals from 177 career games for The Reds. His heaviest return coming in the 1937-38 campaign, his last as a Liverpool player. Little wonder that from his debut in January 1933 he remained a fixture in the side for over five years. Only injury during the 1935-36 season limiting his appearances. He left Anfield to take on the challenge of becoming South Liverpool's player/manager. He held similar posts at Shelbourne United and Ellesmere Port.

Alan Hansen

It could all have turned out differently for the tall Scot as football wasn't the only sport he excelled at. Volleyball and basketball could also have earned him international honours.

Doubtless he would have been equally as good in his original day job - accountancy. As it turned out number crunching's loss was football's gain. After

Alan Hansen - Central defender considered by Liverpool fans to be the best in the world.
He signed from Partick Thistle just before Liverpool's first European Cup win but had to wait until the
following season until he was given his chance.

a couple of seasons with Partick Thistle the young defender caught Bob Paisley's eye. He joined Liverpool just before the 1977 European Cup Final but had to wait until the following season to make his debut. Over the next term he became a first team regular and never looked back. Kenny Dalglish made him captain at the beginning of his stint as manager but in truth he always led by example.

An ability to read the game and positional sense gave him the edge over most attackers. He was just as classy coming forward when necessary and scored a fair amount of goals - some vital ones. The only question mark over his entire career was why Scotland only saw fit to cap him 26 times. This did not trouble the club or the fans who realised his true worth.

He retired from the professional game seven days after his great friend Kenny Dalglish resigned as team boss in February 1991 drawing a curtain on an outstanding career spanning almost 700 first team games and bringing a very disappointing week for every Liverpool fan to an end.

Sam Hardy

The princely sum of £500 exchanged hands between Liverpool and Chesterfield for a 'keeper who a few months earlier had visited Anfield for the first time and conceded six goals.

His performances for Liverpool suggested that the Chesterfield game was either a temporary blip or simply down to the skill of he opposition. He spent six happy seasons on Merseyside and claimed a championship winners medal in his first season. In 239 league and cup games for the club he kept 63 clean sheets. He was also awarded England international caps while a Liverpool player. International recognition continued after his departure for Villa Park in 1912. He won two FA Cup winners' medals during his time with the Midlands side.

Steve Harkness

At 18 years of age when signed by Kenny Dalglish in July 1989 Steve Harkness was one for the future. Having captained the England youth side and played just 13 games for Carlisle United, The Reds' boss was taking a gamble even if the stake was a relatively modest £75,000. There was little chance of the Cumbrian being given an immediate chance and it was two years before he graduated to the first team. The run was brief and followed only by more small opportunities.

Loan transfers to Huddersfield Town and Southend United then managed by former Liverpool midfielder Ronnie Whelan during the 1993-94 and 1994-5 seasons respectively, did at least provide more first team action, and more importantly, experience. Still there seemed no way in and the thought of a permanent move from Anfield rather than one just lasting a month or two cropped up in Steve's mind. But Stig Inge Bjornebye breaking his leg late in 1995 freed up the left back spot once more and for a length of time allowed the youngster to show exactly how he had matured as a player over the years.

By this time Liverpool had adopted a 3-5-2 formation with the full-backs invited to support the attack at every opportunity. It was a role Harkness excelled in and made it almost impossible for the manager to drop him.

Suspension and injury - ironically a broken leg, the injury which gave him his initial chance - ended his season. A comeback was made in the centre of defence and continued once all three first choice centre-halfs returned at his preferred left-back berth.

An offer to join former boss Graeme Souness at Benfica proved tempting and ended his stay on Merseyside after close to 200 games for The Reds. Similar to a lot of English imports shipped out by the former Liverpool boss the move went sour when the man who signed them left. A return to the domestic game came with Blackburn Rovers who Souness would later join as manager.

Jim Harley

Few players boasted the pace of the Liverpool full-back but few players were also champion sprinters in their youth. As an 18 year old he was competing in and winning numerous professional races under the assumed name of A.B. Mitchell due to the strict rules governing sports, and especially athletics, at the time.

The Scotsman played lower grade football with Hearts o'Beath before accepting the offer of a contract with The Reds. It took time to shift the likes of Tom Cooper from the starting eleven and over his first two seasons he managed just 12 outings as cover. A chance to establish a foothold came in the shape of injury to Cooper combined with a small scale selection crisis at left back. Harley switched between the two positions with consummate ease managing to make 33 appearances and remained an integral part of the side until the outbreak of war in September 1939.

He was sent off in Liverpool's last game before the hostilities started but turned out for the club in the various competitions set up while the Football League was suspended. Six years later he was still with The Reds making 17 appearances throughout the 1946-47 championship winning season. He had reassumed possession of his place the following season but was forced to retire half way through the campaign.

Jimmy Harrower

Although bought as a piece of a jigsaw that was deemed worthy enough to win Liverpool promotion back to the top flight, life never worked out like that for either the player or club. Manager Phil Taylor spotted the midfielder who had made 36 league appearances for Hibernian over two seasons.

He was one of the most naturally gifted inside-forwards in the British game able to hold the ball under great pressure due to his sheer strength, retain possession thanks to a host of tricks and raw ability and provide a high percentage of accurate passes which could split even the tightest of defences. Though not as fast as some of his contemporaries nor possessing the greatest of shots he was nonetheless a great asset to the side.

Despite commanding displays towards the close of his first half season with The Reds, Liverpool could finish no better than fourth. A position the club occupied 12 months later.

Consecutive third place finishes over his next two seasons with the club made it a case of 'so near yet so far' in terms of that return to Division One and Harrower's lack of consistency was seen as a huge factor in this failure. All too often he would meander his way through games, still pretty to watch but lacking the cutting edge which was so evident at other times.

He was given a fair chance under Bill Shankly who, like his predecessor, saw and admired what could be on offer if only his talent could be reharnessed. Harrower was even tried along various points of midfield and attack. An alternative school of thought was that he became unnecessarily blamed for Liverpool's inability to gain promotion. The fact that he was such a flair player and not an honest toiler undermined the true level of his contribution. Be that as it may he was allowed to join Newcastle United for £15,000 in 1961.

Hat-Tricks

William Miller was the first Liverpool player to score a hat-trick in the initial qualifying round of the 1892-93 FA Cup against Nantwich in a 4-0 win on 15th October. One week later in the Lancashire League he was at it again recording another treble in the 5-0 demolition of Higher Walton. Ian Callaghan notched the club's first League Cup hat-trick in a 4th Round replay at home to Hull City in December 1973. The first player to hit three goals in a European competition was Alun Evans in his heroic performance against Bayern Munich in the Quarter Final 1st leg of the 1970-71 European Fairs Cup.

The number of players who have notched hat-tricks on their debuts are very small in number. Antonio Rowley was never a first team regular but staked a good claim for a starting berth in the opening game of the 1954-55 season. He bagged three in just under half an hour - including two in the last four minutes - as Liverpool pipped Doncaster Rovers 3-2. The fastest hat-trick scored by any Liverpool player came in 4 minutes and 33 seconds when Robbie Fowler's strike demolished Arsenal at Anfield on August 28th 1994. It is also the fastest treble in Premiership history.

Tony Hateley

80 goals in 150 games for Notts County and 86 in 148 appearances for Aston Villa marked Tony Hateley out as a feared and respected striker. He was enjoying a charmed career until the tail end of the 1965-66 season when after being selected for Alf Ramsey's World Cup squad he was forced to withdraw from the party due to injury.

He had signed for Chelsea before Bill Shankly decided to make his move. It was common knowledge that he had failed to settle in at Stamford Bridge, so when the chance to join Liverpool came along there was no hesitation.

The £96,000 shelled out for him paid instant dividends when, in his third game, he scored a hat-trick in a 6-0 defeat of Newcastle United. That first season saw him crack 27 goals in 52 games. However, injury ravaged him once more and just weeks into the next season he signed for Coventry City.

Steve Heighway

A graduate of Warwick University Steve Heighway earned first class honours at the Anfield Soccer Academy. Although he turned out for Manchester City as an amateur the Maine Road club never took him on professional terms. When Liverpool spotted him he was playing non-league football with Skelmersdale United. Scouts raved over his performances but it was Bob Paisley's sons, Robert and Graham, who suggested that their Dad had a look at him. Bob was so impressed that he wasted little time persuading Bill Shankly to snap him up. He scored on his home debut in a 2-0 win over Burnley. Despite his late arrival to the professional ranks he earned just about every honour possible plus more than 30 caps for the Republic of Ireland.

On leaving Anfield he took up a place with The Minnesota Kicks in the North American Soccer League. He returned and took the post of Youth Development Officer where his tenure has proved to be a complete success. The Irishman's tutelage has reaped a promising crop of current first teamers and has seen many more talented players earmarked for the future.

Joe Hewitt

When long serving members of Liverpool's staff are mentioned thoughts automatically turn to those who started out as players and ended up as coaches or who served in some other behind-the-scenes capacity. Familiar names such as Paisley, Moran and Evans roll off the tongue. One that doesn't is that of Joe Hewitt who was part of the Anfield set-up for an incredible 60 years. Like many players during the early years of the 1900s he was recruited from Sunderland but took his time to justify his recruitment thanks to an injury which kept him out for all but nine games of the 1904-05 2nd Division Championship winning sea-

Steve Heighway trod an unorthodox road towards professional football and was only persuaded to ditch his plans to teach after completing his university education. He is currently Liverpool's head of Youth Development.

son. However, when Liverpool claimed the English championship the following season he missed just one game and contributed 23 goals - more than twice as many as any other player could manage. Injury cursed the number of games he was able to play as The Reds unsuccessfully set about defending their crown but he was back in business once more with 21 strikes from 36 games.

Had his time at Anfield been blessed with a little more fortune it seems he would have been a certainty to reach a century of goals and a double century of appearances for the club but by the time the curtain was drawn on his stay with the club in December 1909 he had scored 69 from 164 games. Bolton Wanderers were happy to take a chance on the player that had proved slightly injury prone over recent seasons but the gamble backfired. Further physical trouble ended his professional career after a few short months at Burnden Park. He returned to Anfield in a coaching capacity seeing out the remainder of his employment with Liverpool as a handyman.

Heysel Stadium

With the exception of the Hillsborough Disaster in 1989 the crowd rioting at the 1984 European Cup Final marks the blackest chapter in the club's history. 39 fans were killed. 38 were supporters of the Italian club Juventus.

The incident, along with a list of hooligan related disturbances over many years by English clubs and the national side, prompted UEFA to ban all the country's sides from European competition. For a spell English clubs weren't even allowed to play outside the UK. The ban was relaxed in 1990 but Liverpool had to wait another year to be reinstated.

The Hillsborough Disaster

No Liverpool fan, indeed no football fan, can claim to have been left untouched by the events of 15th April 1989. 96 Liverpool fans lost their lives as a result of crushing in the pens at the Leepings Lane End of the Hillsborough Ground. The FA Cup semi-final with Nottingham Forest was abandoned after six minutes due to the tragedy.

In what many see as a fitting tribute to those who died The Reds won the cup after a highly emotional game with Everton. In the years that have followed many questions remain unanswered and some individuals are still seen as unaccountable for their actions. As a result a campaign for justice continues to gather momentum.

Gordon Hodgson

A pivotal member of South African Amateur's touring party in 1925, Gordon Hodgson decided to chance his arm and stay in Britain. A number of impressive displays earned him the offer of a professional contract with Liverpool and made him a first choice selection almost as soon as he arrived. He never looked back and enjoyed a highly successful career on Merseyside.

That was no shock considering he was a robust inside forward who scored more goals than any Liverpool player ever had. 240 in 378 games is a strong testament to his abilities in that department.

He proved such a hit in his adoptive land that he even earned three England caps. His 36 goals in the 1930-31 campaign was a record tally for a league season which took Roger Hunt the best part of 30 years to break. He hit four hat-tricks that term including four goals in the 5-3 whacking of Sheffield Wednesday.

He was still averaging a goal every other game when he was transferred to Leeds United just before Christmas in 1935. It could have been seen as a shock move as he had set a blistering pace during the opening part of the season netting 9 times in 15 games.

However, The Reds were able to call upon an impressive array of strikers who were just as talented and in equally impressive form. After retiring he took the manager's job at Port Vale. He died in 1951 whilst in the post.

Honours

League Division 1 Champions:	1900-01	1905-06	1921-22
	1922-23	1946-47	1963-64
	1965-66	1972-73	1975-76
	1976-77	1978-79	1979-80
	1981-82	1982-83	1983-84
	1985-86	1987-88	1989-90
(Record of 18 League Championships)			
League Division 2 Champions:	1893-94	1895-96	1904-05
	1961-62		
FA Cup Winners:	1965	1974	1986
	1989	1992	2001
League Cup Winners:	1981	1982	1983
	1984	1995	2001
(Record of 7 victories)	2003		
European Cup Winners:	1976-77	1977-78	1980-81
	1983-84		
UEFA Cup Winners:	1972-73	1975-76	2000-01
Super Cup Winners:	1977		

Fred Hopkin

This recruit from Old Trafford could honestly say his first goal for Liverpool set the stadium alight. Seconds after he netted the final goal in a 3-0 win over Bolton Wanderers in March 1923, the old Main Stand was ablaze. That was his 70th league appearance for The Reds. His goal scoring record never reached the dizzy heights after that. In his 359 career games for the club he netted just 11 times.

Ray Houghton

The Glasgow born midfielder became an Irish international, due to the birth place of his father. He started out with West Ham United as a trainee but after just one appearance he shifted across London to Fulham where he spent three seasons before joining Oxford United. It was at the Manor Ground that Ray became one of the most sought after players in England. Liverpool had Craig Johnston in that right sided position and were already cruising to the league title after recording eight victories and one draw in the nine games played before he joined. Not content Kenny Dalglish decided he wanted the best in every department and this included the winger who was bought for £875,000 during October. A busy looking player who enjoyed running at defenders he also quite liked beating his foes before sending in a cross or shot. A different type of player from John Barnes on the left flank who carried out his job in a far more simple way. He was nonetheless a perfect balance to the Jamaican and played just as big a part in The Reds' success.

Before joining Liverpool he had only a League Cup winner's medal to show for his seven seasons in the game. Just over 12 months after arriving at Anfield, he had a league championship and an FA Cup winner's medal and was again a vital member of the side which almost secured the title once more. Another year after that he and his colleagues atoned for although Ray missed a large proportion of the campaign with injury managing just 16 starts and five appearances as a substitute. While his performances may not have been as solid as they had in the three previous seasons, Houghton was The Reds' best player over two very inconsistent seasons that followed. Despite winning a further FA Cup Liverpool were a shadow of the team that had dominated the game in previous seasons. Hence the surprise when Graeme Souness allowed him to join Aston Villa for a little less than he was bought for in July 1992 after almost 200 games in a Liverpool shirt.

Ray Houghton, a Glasgow born Irish international joined the all-conquering 1987-88 Liverpool team. He provided the final piece of a jigsaw which Kenny Dalglish had been striving to assemble since taking charge of the club.

John Houlding

Liverpool Football Club's founding father became a very wealthy man due to an amazing business acumen which saw him turn a modest public house in to a brewing empire. He was also a prominent city councillor and served as Mayor. Before Liverpool Football Club even existed he was Everton's benefactor and ensured that they were fit and financially sound enough to join the newly formed Football League. The well documented rift led him to form Liverpool in 1892. Although still involved with the club he virtually stood aside to concentrate on his political career allowing his great friend and protégé John McKenna to run affairs.

Gerard Houllier

By the time Gerard Houllier, who had masterminded the French national side's rise to World and European Champions, was ready to return to club management, there was a clamour to attract his services. Tottenham Hotspur and Sheffield Wednesday were the front runners for a long time. Hillsborough seemed to be his destination before Liverpool emerged from the shadows as a surprise choice. Surprise because The Reds already had a manager in Roy Evans. Houllier was appointed as joint boss working alongside the present incumbent in a move which many saw as a sacking for Evans. The lure of a return to Liverpool, the city where Houllier taught in a school in Walton during the late 1960s, was too much to resist.

The two remained in joint control until November 1998 when a run of bad results caused the Anfield stalwart to revise his position leaving Houllier in sole control. Given his own way Houllier proved ruthless in shaping the side into his own. High profile players such as Paul Ince were released and a number of new players brought in to the fold. Liverpool struggled for the remainder of the campaign and indifferent results led to a relatively low placed finish. The following season saw The Reds fail to make for The UEFA Champions' League after looking dead certs to finish in the third and final qualifying place. Liverpool failed to score in any of their final five games. A 1-0 defeat away to Bradford City, who needed the win to secure their own future in The Premier League, ended the club's chances on the final day of the season.

Twelve months later that disappointment was reversed as Liverpool not only claimed third place in the league but pulled off a unique Cup treble. The winning of trophies wasn't something new to the Frenchman who, after finishing his career as a teacher, joined Le Touquet in 1973 as a player/coach. Further positions were held at Arras and Noeux Les Mines.

A chance to manage a major club came when he was offered the top job at Lens. Although major honours eluded him over his three years in charge it was clear that he was a man more than able to succeed at this level. A fact proved when he guided Paris St.Germain to the French title in 1986.

Earmarked for service by his country he became the French FA's Technical Director and assistant to the national team boss. He was subsequently named head coach but resigned from his post in 1994 when France failed to gain qualification for the World Cup finals held in the USA. However, he remained part of the set up taking charge at youth level and leading his charges to European

Under-18 Championship in 1996. He took the Under-20s side to the quarter-finals of their World Championships 12 months later. His abilities are so well respected that he became a long serving member of the UEFA and FIFA Technical Committees. His involvement in team affairs was temporarily disrupted when he was taken ill during a home game with Leeds United. A serious heart condition was diagnosed and operated on.

A matter of months later he was back in full control of the side though had never really took a complete sabbatical and was said to be in almost daily contact with his assistant Phil Thompson very early on in his recuperation. After guiding The Reds to their highest final placing in the Premiership in May 2002 Gerard Houllier has found the early success hard to recapture. A Worthington Cup success over Manchester United aside he has seen his side seemingly lose ground on rivals.

Emlyn Hughes

Despite a handful of appearances for Blackpool The Reds handed over the £65,000 fee they had negotiated with the Seasiders in a very confident mood. Bill Shankly saw him as the best exponent of the centre back's art he had seen in some time. Hughes' enthusiasm for the cause was infectious, and the supporters loved him. If The Reds needed it he would run himself into the ground for them.

His many sorties up front earned him almost 50 goals for the club. As captain during the 1976-77 season he had the distinction of becoming the first Liverpool player to lay his hands on the European Cup. After almost a decade at Anfield he signed for Wolverhampton Wanderers where he added a League Cup winners medal to his bulging collection of honours.

He won no less than nine domestic and European trophies with The Reds and he captained England in 40 of his 62 international appearances. He was capped 59 times as a Liverpool player.

Laurie Hughes

Recruited from Tranmere Rovers for whom he played as an amateur Laurie Hughes was a shrewd addition to the Liverpool side made during the Second World War. It was almost three years before he could make an official debut for the club in the 1945-46 FA Cup competition and a further season before he could turn out in a Football League game. A championship medal was secured thanks to 30 appearances. His height made him a commanding presence in the air and his ability to control the game from midfield, due to clever understanding of play was another attribute which ensured he stayed an

Nicknamed 'Crazy Horse' by The Kop as a result of his galloping style and eager attitude Emlyn Hughes went on to captain Liverpool and England. A role in which he became the first Reds skipper to lift the European Cup.

Anfield regular for 12 seasons. Only during the 1948-49 and 1952-53 seasons did he play less than half the games on offer and in both seasons this absence was due to injury.

International honours came as a matter of course but were limited to the three games England mustered during the 1950 World Cup tournament. At club level the next high point after the title win was the 1950 FA Cup final. A broken toe had kept him out of the semi-final with Everton and a few league games but when Liverpool made their first appearance at Wembley Hughes was preferred to the man who had scored one of the goals that had brought The Reds to the twin towers. Bob Paisley had to make way. Within four seasons Liverpool had been relegated. Dick White was providing stiff competition for his place by the turn of the 1957-58 season and despite missing a single game throughout the previous campaign the Waterloo born midfielder made just one more appearance as part of the sorry eleven that were hammered 5-1 by Charlton Athletic. The chance being handed to him by a bout of Asian Flu that had struck the playing staff and forced seven changes over the previous two games.

Roger Hunt

Immediately before joining Liverpool in the late 50's Roger Hunt had earned rave reviews while appearing for The British Army. Even though The Reds were his first professional club his strengths and ability to crack it at the highest level were obvious. He was tremendously athletic, strong and held such a high level of stamina which allowed him to cover ground with consummate ease over 90 minutes.

His goal scoring record was second to none. Even when compared to the greats of both his day and the years which have followed. The fact that it took almost 30 years for some of his achievements to be surpassed is proof of that. A debut goal in a home win over Scunthorpe United showed the shape of things to come. He netted a further 20 times during that first season and was virtually the first choice striker from then on spearheading the push for promotion and ultimately the quest to become England's best. The opening goal of the 1965 Cup Final was one of the greatest moments of his club career and Liverpool's first in the showpiece occasion. The 245 league goals and 285 times he scored for Liverpool in total have only been surpassed by Ian Rush. Away from the domestic game he earned the distinction of a World Cup Winner's Medal with England in 1966. In recognition of his achievement The Kop christened him Sir Roger.

I

Paul Ince

Had Liverpool rather than Manchester United signed the combative midfielder from West Ham in 1989 there seems little doubt that The Reds would have continued to dominate the domestic game. While Ince was leading the Old Trafford club's charge for honours with his commanding displays in the middle of the park Anfield could have used the qualities of a midfield general. The control exacted by Ince was something Liverpool hadn't held since the departure of Steve McMahon and before him Graeme Souness. Of the two former Reds Essex born Ince was more comparable to Souness. Had the two competed during the same generation fans of blood sports would have craved match day tickets. The thunderous style both exerted on all those around them could be a chilling spectacle. Not to say either were not skilful footballers. Ince was as composed on the ball as any other player in his position it was just that the edge he provided could make the difference between winning and losing.

After two seasons doing the same job for Inter Milan in Serie A Ince was ready to come home but very few clubs seemed to follow up their interest with a genuine bid for a world class player still the right side of 30. Liverpool had been linked for months but negotiations over a fee and personal terms dragged the move out. Whilst not the force that had visited Anfield during his days with United, he managed to bring that much needed steel to his side but at first seemed not to probe as much as he once did. However, alongside Jamie Redknapp a formidable partnership looked likely to raise The Reds to better things. In tandem the two set about imposing Liverpool's rhythm on the game. It was a task they enjoyed great success in as they formed an understanding with few parallels. The pairing was interrupted by injury to both players then abruptly ended when, despite retaining his services both as a player and as captain after taking sole charge of the club, Gerrard Houllier told Ince that he should seek another employer in the summer of 1999 as his chances of a start at Anfield were virtually nil. A bitter Ince moved to Middlesbrough not long after.

Injuries

Wayne Harrison signed for Liverpool at the age of 17 - the £250,000 fee was a record for a teenager. His displays in the junior ranks at Oldham Athletic persuaded Joe Fagan part with the money. It was the late 80's and unfortunately for the youngster Anfield had a long list of quality strikers. Progress to the first team would be difficult if not impossible, and, with the exception of a few run outs in pre-season friendlies it proved to be exactly that. The youngster continued to score goals in the reserves but never got the break he deserved. It was while playing for the second string that he suffered the agonising knee injury which eventually ended his professional career aged 23.

With more than a century of appearances for his hometown club, Bristol Rovers, behind him, Nicky Tanner's career seemed to be taking a nose dive. He was close to agreeing terms with Fourth Division Torquay United when Kenny Dalglish offered him the chance to play for the League Champions in July 1988. His debut came a year or so later with a late run off the bench in a 4-1 win against Manchester City around Christmas 1989. Breaking in to the rock solid Red's defence seemed an unattainable goal. However, loan spells with Norwich City and Swindon Town served as a good base when a glut of injuries forced Graeme Souness to blood many of his reserves and youngsters. At the close of the 1991-92 campaign he had made 45 appearances in all competitions. He made the most of his chances but saw a serious knee injury dash all his hopes the following season. Despite months of fighting to regain his fitness it eventually led to the end of his career in 1994.

Michael Stensgaard was Roy Evans' first signing for a nominal fee in July 1994 from the same Danish club which cultivated the young Peter Schmeichel's talents - Hvidovre. He was already a Danish U-21 international, but he hardly made the bench for The Reds due to a catalogue of injuries. This forced the manager to take a couple of 'keepers on loan and put youth team keeper Tony Warner in the deputy's role. When he came back from the original setback he dislocated an already weak shoulder and a few weeks prior to the start of the 1996/97 campaign announced that the injury had forced a premature retirement from the game. He returned to Denmark to coach young 'keepers at his former club but did manage a limited comeback eventually joining Southampton.

Inter City Fairs Cup

The Inter City Fairs Cup was the precursor to the UEFA Cup. Liverpool qualified on four occasions but their progress was poor. It wasn't until their final attempt to bring the trophy back to Merseyside during the 1970-71 season that the club managed to pass the third round stage. Bill Shankly's men made impressive tracks towards the semi-finals where Leeds Utd provided the opposition. Although the two clubs had battled it out for domestic supremacy for a few seasons, it was the first time The Reds had met an English club in Europe. A shock 1-0 defeat at Anfield proved Liverpool's undoing as the 2nd leg at Elland Road finished goalless.

Internationals

Apart from the home nations Liverpool have acquired talent from many different countries and almost every continent. Countries represented include the Republic of Ireland, Norway, Iceland, Sweden, Holland, Hungary, Germany, Croatia, France, The Czech Republic, Finland, Denmark, Portugal and Switzerland. Other Liverpool players have received full international caps from Australia, Cameroon, Gineau, Zimbabwe, South Africa, The United States of America and Israel.

The four international federations of the United Kingdom have been able to select from a rich pool of talent at the club. Harry Bradshaw was the first man from Anfield to turn out for England duty when Ireland visited Nottingham on 20th February 1897. There was an easy 6-0 win for the hosts. Roger Hunt and Ian Callaghan were both members of the 1966 World Cup squad but only Roger played in the final. Cally's only run out during the competition came against France in the group stages. In recent times Ray Clemence, Emlyn Hughes, Kevin Keegan, Phil Neal, Phil Thompson, Paul Ince and Michael Owen have all led their country while playing for Liverpool. Emile Heskey and Jamie Carragher became makeshift skippers in the summer of 2003 albeit for a matter of minutes.

Of the many Scots to have plied their trade on the red half of Merseyside Kenny Dalglish is by far the most prolific. Not only is he the most capped player in Scotland's proud history he is also the joint highest goalscorer. Along with Graeme Souness the legendary striker is the only Liverpool man to have captained the Tartan Army. George Allan was the first Red to don the dark blue of his homeland when Scotland took on their oldest foes, England, at Crystal Palace on 3rd April 1897. George went back to Anfield a happy man following a 2-1 win for his side.

Maurice Parry had to settle for a 1-1 draw when Scotland visited Wrexham on 2nd March 1901. He became the first Liverpudlian Welsh Dragon when the country of his birth awarded him a cap. Ian Rush is the only man in recent times to have worn the captain's armband and the club's most capped Welshman. 67 of his 73 appearances for Wales came as a Liverpool player.

Before Northern Ireland and the Republic of Ireland went their separate ways in 1924 players from the Emerald Isle would turn out for Ireland. The first man to do so was Bill Lacey on 18th January 1913 when Belfast hosted a

1-0 win for Wales. The first Liverpool man to play for the newly formed Northern Ireland was Elisha Scott. Wales were the opposition once more and Elisha kept a clean sheet in a 0-0 draw.

During the war Victory and Wartime Internationals took place. Jack Balmer and Ephraim Longworth turned out for England, Scotland called upon the services of Matt Busby, Willie Fagan, Jim Harley and Billy Liddell and Ray Lambert and Robert Matthews were selected by Wales.

Kevin Keegan and John Toshack are the only former Liverpool players to manage home international sides but Peter Cormack had a spell as Botswana's national coach.

J

Brian Jackson

Unlike their modern day equivalents teenage players were not supposed to cost too large a fee. However, the £7,000 it took to tempt 18 year old Brian Jackson away from Leyton Orient in November 1951 was large enough to raise eyebrows. He paid a quick return on his investment scoring on his debut against Bolton Wanderers just past the hour mark to earn The Reds a point. That was his only goal for just over a season as he was largely left out of the picture for a year and only began to force himself back into the frame during Liverpool's 1953-54 season when the club were unceremoniously relegated. Despite his obvious talents he remained a bit part player for the next four seasons and never managed to appear in more than half the games. Consequently a frustrated player made his exit in July 1958 for Port Vale. How much his experiences at Anfield shaped the remainder of his career may well never be known as he struggled to hold down his place at Vale Park. He moved on to Peterborough United, Lincoln City and non-league Burton Albion before finally calling it a day.

David James

Without doubt one of the most gifted 'keepers of recent years he was also the most gaffe prone as was highlighted many times during his days at Anfield. There were clear consequences with regards to his performance, as the errors received more and more attention under the media spotlight. They intensified in his own mind and had a habit of repeating themselves.

A certain tactical naïveté was evident in his early days with The Reds but once coached in the ways of his craft he seemed to be making progress and was capped by England in 1997.

He had hung in to unseat Bruce Grobbelaar as the number one and saw off Mike Hooper who had decided that fresh pastures provided his best chance of first team action. A succession of loan 'keepers provided cover but with just youth 'keepers and untried deputies he retained his place as Roy Evans kept confidence in a man he seemed sure would eventually come good.

The departure of Grobbelaar seemed to bring out the best in him, as he grew more assured of his place his performances improved. There were still errors but they were fewer in number and not quite as calamitous. In fact he turned into something of a match winner pulling off save after save during some games and when Liverpool lifted The League Cup in 1995 the 2-1 win owed as much to their keeper as it did to anyone else. However, despite persevering with James when he first took sole charge of team affairs Gerrard Houllier was less than impressed. He already had one keeper to pressurise him in the shape of Brad Friedel but decided that both were not the right man for the job and that David would be allowed to leave during the summer of 1999 when a decent offer came in. As Europe was scoured for a replacement, John Gregory at Aston Villa paid £1.8 million for his services. As Sander Westerveld was drafted in during the summer of 2001 he moved to London in order to play for West Ham United.

David Johnson

Although David Johnson was signed from Ipswich Town he started his career as an apprentice at Everton. Following John Toshack's departure he managed to claim the vacant centre forward's role and formed a formidable partnership with Kenny Dalglish during the 1978-79 season. He finished as top scorer with 21 goals from 37 appearances. Ian Rush's arrival led to a very quick demise in his Anfield fortunes and eventually to a Goodison Park return in August 1982.

Despite playing an in and out role at the club his trophy haul is enviable and includes four league championships, three European Cups (although two were as a non-playing substitute) and a League Cup Winners medal (this time as a participating substitute in the 1982 final). He earned a respectable eight England caps during his time at Anfield and scored a brace in a 3-1 defeat of Argentina. Just before ending his career with Preston North End he became another former Liverpudlian attracted to the prospect of playing in America.

Craig Johnston

Lake McQuarrie and Sydney City provided a showcase for this South African's ability. Clubs from various countries came to watch him and professional terms at Middlesbrough tempted him to ply his trade half way around the world. Joe Fagan paid over £600,000 to bring him to Anfield in 1981. It was a lot of money and the relationship between player and manager was often strained causing all manner of transfer speculation. Whatever the truth of those rumours Johnston was still there when Kenny Dalglish took the manager's hot seat. In total contrast to his previous form, which could best be described as patchy, Johnston blossomed under the Scotsman's leadership, making himself a pivotal member of the 1985-86 double winning side.

Although David Johnson was a boyhood fan of Liverpool he turned out for Everton and scored against The Reds before he joined Ipswich Town. Liverpool signed him from the Portman Road club before the 1976-77 season for a fee of £200,000 a club record. During the campaign he became the first player to score for both clubs in the Merseyside Derby.

Craig Johnston retired from the game at the age of 27 with much to contribute.
A high octane style endeared him to the fans.

Ray Houghton's arrival limited his first team run outs and at the age of 27 he retired from the game. His sister had suffered serious injuries in an accident and 'Skippy' as the fans had come to call him returned home to care for her following the 1988 cup final.

His boundless enthusiasm on the pitch was mirrored off it. Song writing, surfing and photography are among his many hobbies. He also devised a game show syndicated on TV stations around the world - The Main Event and pioneered the revolutionary Adidas Predator boot worn by many top players. He now holds a senior executive position with Liverpool sports kit manufacturer Reebok.

Joey Jones

Despite a relatively short three season stay with the club Joey established himself as a crowd favourite due to the clenched fist salute he used to give the fans in times of glory. He joined just before the 1975-76 season in a move which was thought likely to threaten Tommy Smith's place in the team. When he left Anfield it was for a return to the club he left -Wrexham. Apart from brief stints with Chelsea and Huddersfield Town he remained with the North Wales outfit until he hung up his boots in the mid 90's.

Rob Jones

Had Lady Luck smiled on Rob Jones it seems there would have been no limit to what he could have achieved. A graduate of Dario Gradi's school of excellence at Crewe Alexandra his rise was as meteoric as it was unheralded. At a tender 19 years of age he was signed by Graeme Souness in October 1991 for an initial £300,000. There were further payments to be triggered by other events. An extra £150,000 would wing its way to Gresty Road when he played 20 first team games and in the event of winning five international caps the fee would rise by another £50,000.

Though born in the North Wales town of Wrexham, England was his chosen country and youth honours had already been achieved. Those extra funds were delivered far swifter than anyone would have imagined possible. His debut was on no less a stage than Old Trafford two days after joining The Reds and his performance in the 0-0 draw was more than creditable.

Within a further five months he was awarded that first full England cap. A few weeks later Crewe had their extra £150,000 and but for shin splints they would surely have received the balance of the deal but a summer of rest meant there would be no chance to add to his tally of games for England.

Though he had grown from a lower league footballer to England international and FA Cup winner in just over half a year there was little time to rest on his laurels. Competition for places was tough and past glory meant nothing at Anfield, it was what a player managed in the present that counted.

He fitted well into the new wing-back system introduced by Roy Evans proving a willing runner and adept crosser of the ball. Thereafter, life proved a little more difficult. Jason McAteer was bought and while not initially viewed as competition he covered at right-back during the bouts of injury which still plagued Jones.

One of those was a back problem that could have ended his career following the 1995-96 season and he was ordered to rest for six months otherwise risk not just retirement but a crippling condition that would limit his day to day activity let alone football.

Chances were limited due to the form of McAteer and others but when an opportunity did arise it seemed that another injury scare would strike and rule him out once more. Moves to other clubs home and abroad were rumoured but never materialised. Once his contract ran out in 1999 Rob Jones was released as a free agent and despite a trial at West Ham United the opportunity was scuppered by further setbacks.

K

Kevin Keegan

When Bill Shankly brought this unassuming youngster to Merseyside there were many who wondered whether he could recreate the promise he had shown in the 4th Division at the highest level. A host of top flight clubs had him watched but Joe Fagan and Bob Paisley decided they had seen enough after 20 minutes of their scouting trip. With a recommendation like that there was little other option than to sign him. The initial plan was that he should take over from Ian Callaghan on the right hand side of midfield. A cartilage operation had left the veteran struggling for fitness. As it happened Cally not only made a full recovery, his career enjoyed something of an Indian summer. As a consequence Keegan was placed up front where he formed a devastating partnership with John Toshack.

He scored two goals in the 1974 FA Cup final and the first leg of the 1973 UEFA Cup Final. He notched efforts in both legs of the 1976 competition. Continental clubs were rumoured to be taking a keen interest in his services, but SV Hamburg was the club who managed to land him. He returned to these shores a few years later and joined Southampton.

Two years after his arrival at The Dell he began a love affair with Newcastle United. Terry McDermott was tempted back to the club and in their first full season together The Magpies were promoted to Division One.

He retired from the game at the end of the 1983-84 season. A 4-0 FA cup defeat by Liverpool in a 3rd Round tie at Anfield convinced him that this season would be his last.

The Kemlyn Road Stand

The original stand was altered in 1963 when it became an all seated grandstand with a cantilevered design and an increased capacity of 6,700. The cost was a cool £350,000. Plans to build executive boxes during the early 1980's were postponed as the club felt the economic downturn at the time didn't warrant the expense. Talk of further development to the stand gathered speed in the wake of The Taylor Report and it became the first Anfield stand to be upgraded in line with his Lordship's recommendations. The original seating remained

A dynamic player who starred for both club and country throughout the 1970s, Kevin Keegan decided to chance his luck abroad after Liverpool won the European Cup for the first time in May 1977.

but the executive boxes considered just over a decade earlier were installed. A further tier of seating was built. The finished stand was opened to the public in the early part of the 1992-93 season. An official ceremony was performed a few months later by Leonard Jouhansen before a league game with Southampton. Given the year of its revamp - the club's 100th - the decision to call it The Centenary Stand was made.

Alan Kennedy, affectionately nicknamed 'Barney Rubble' after the cartoon character from The Flinstones remained Liverpool's first choice right back for seven seasons.

Alan Kennedy

A solid left back who scored his fair share of goals, more often than not vital cup winning ones, on his many forays upfield. The 1984 European Cup Final penalty was a classic example of his nerve. Three years earlier he scored the goal which won the 1981 competition. That solitary strike was The Reds' margin of victory over Real Madrid. He also netted the equaliser in the 1984 League Cup triumph over Manchester United allowing the game to proceed to

Ray Kennedy had already won the League and FA Cup double with Arsenal when he joined Liverpool but went on to further glory at Anfield. His signing was announced at the same press conference which Bill Shankly publicised his plans for retirement.

extra-time when Ronnie Whelan got the winner. His influence in the Liverpool defence was stoical due to his rugged style, tough tackling and ability to interpret play.

Ray Kennedy

As Bill Shankly's last signing Ray Kennedy had ensured a place in the club's record books before he even kicked a ball in their name. He proved a magnificent legacy for the great man to leave. He was a key member of Arsenal's 1970-71 double winning squad. At Highbury he was used exclusively as a striker but Bob Paisley moved him over to the left side of midfield. His goal scoring record with The Gunners matched any other forward in the land. He found the net with slightly less regularity at Anfield but it was the overall effort he brought to the side that made him the success he was on Merseyside. He recreated himself into a devastatingly creative player in the middle of the park supplying many chances for himself and his colleagues.

The Kop

As a reward for its unswerving support over the first few years of its existence and especially during the 1905-06 championship season the Liverpool board decided to build a terraced stand worthy of the loyal fans who gathered behind the goal at the Walton Breck Road end of the ground. It was originally known as the Oakfield Road Embankment or Walton Breck Bank. The imposing mound of stone, cinders, rubble and earth made its debut with a low key 1-0 victory over Stoke City. Ernest Jones, a sports journalist of The Liverpool Daily Post and Echo nicknamed it The Spion Kop - a hill made famous by a bloody battle during the Boer War in 1900. Many soldiers including more than 300 from Merseyside gave their lives in the attempt to secure this strategic point. The name stuck and was officially adopted soon after. It remained largely untouched until 1928 when a roof was added. Further work allowed a boost in capacity.

The terrace measured 394 feet wide and stretched 135 feet from the front to the back and stood 50 feet high allowing almost 30,000 fans to gather on The Kop. Although the supporters' rousing backing of the team had already earned a burgeoning reputation it was at this time that it came into its own. Many clubs have built similar stands over the years and even let them be known as The Kop. However, in the footballing world there is and always be one set of supporters that will spring to mind when the words are mentioned.

An item which still remains from the old stand is the mast of The Great Eastern, one of the first ships to be constructed of iron. The wooden mast was salvaged from a breakers yard and floated across the Mersey from Rock Ferry.

Four Horses carried the huge pole up the Everton Valley to Anfield where it was first erected.

The Taylor Report's suggestions that terracing be replaced by all seated stadium in the top two divisions led to the famous old terrace being demolished at the end of the 1994-95 season. Despite the carnival atmosphere the fans had generated the players failed to live up to the occasion and suffered a disappointing 1-0 defeat to Norwich City. Jeremy Goss was the last player to score at the famous end. At present The Kop Grandstand, as it is now known, appears just as imposing in terms of sheer size, though few would argue that despite the 20,000 or so fans taking their place in the stand each fortnight, seating has quietened crowds not just at Anfield but at grounds up and down the country.

Kop's Last Stand Programme
The match programme issued for the last game before the old terraced Kop was demolished.

L

Bill Lacey

One of the first players to make the journey across Stanley Park following the initial exchanges brought about after the split between Liverpool and Everton. Bill Lacey went on to become a stalwart of The Reds' side in many positions but had struggled to find a place in the Goodison during his three seasons. Although he turned out in many different areas of the field it was as a wing man that he excelled and helped Liverpool reach not only the 1914 FA Cup final but win back to back championships during the 1921-22 and 1922-23 seasons. His skill on the ball and close control being a major factor in these victories. If there was one area in which he could be criticised it was as a goalscorer. He never broke into double figures over a league campaign but five goals in the eight cup games comprising Liverpool's progress to the final against Burnley helped him crack that mark by the close of the 1913-14 campaign. The outbreak of war led him to miss four seasons which would have helped him make well in excess of 300 games for Liverpool. By the time he left to join New Brighton in 1924 he made 257 league and cup outings. He hung up his boots while still with the Wirral based club.

Ray Lambert

The promise shown by Ray Lambert was clear at such an early age that Liverpool set about securing his signature on a contract at the earliest possible opportunity. He was a mere 13 years of age when he signed on the dotted line as an amateur and so impressive was his progress that he was offered a professional contract just over three years later. Capped at schoolboy level he went on to make the grade at senior level. He began his junior career at centre-half but had moved to full-back by the time he made his debut for The Reds over a decade after joining the club. The war rather than form had stopped him making progress but with the Football League suspended he turned out a number of times in the specially arranged competitions that took the place of full time leagues.

As may be expected from such a gifted player he was comfortable on either side of the field and contributed heavily to the form which helped Liverpool win the first post-war championship and reach the 1950 FA Cup final. That The Reds fell from grace and were eventually relegated to the 2nd division was far from the fault of players like Lambert who remained loyal and consistent performers in the cause. He stayed at Anfield until 1956 when he retired at 33 after 20 years' association with Liverpool Football Club.

The Lancashire Cup
A by product of membership of the Lancashire League was entry into the Lancashire Cup. Progress was halted at the 2nd Round stage of the club's one and only entry when local rivals Bootle nudged their way through with a 2-1 win.

The Lancashire League
Liverpool's participation in the league was limited to the club's inaugural season. Once the Football League had rejected an application for membership of the newly formed Second Division, Anfield's directors decided the best way to improve their chances upon future application was to take on the best teams the county had to offer. They were all found wanting as Liverpool cruised to a very comfortable title win. Only Blackpool managed to stave off defeat by the newly formed side. Finishing as champions gave extra impetus to a renewed attempt to gain League status and the bid was subsequently granted. Bootle were the team to make way. The club also won the Liverpool Senior Cup but found success came at a price. Both trophies were stolen and a £130 charge for replacements was levied against them.

The club's record in the league is as follows:

P	W	D	L	F	A	Pts
22	17	2	3	66	19	36

Chris Lawler
A baby faced full back who proved to be one of the most prolific goal scoring defenders the club has ever had. He became a first team regular in the mid 60's. A berth he didn't lose until late November 1973 when injury cost him precious opportunities to challenge Phil Neal and others for his place. He left the club in 1975 to join Ian St John at Portsmouth after notching 61 goals from just under 550 first team appearances. He has remained within the game in various capacities and spent a number of seasons with League of Wales side Porthmadog.

*61 goals from 546 games for The Reds makes Chris Lawler one of the
highest scoring full backs in league history. His scoring record was aided by
his ability to steal into the box virtually unseen and round off moves.*

Tommy Lawrence

Five years as understudy to Tommy Younger, Bert Slater and Jimmy Furnell
proved an excellent learning curve for this young keeper. From making his
debut in October 1962 he was the first choice for duty between the sticks until
Ray Clemence's emergence in 1970. Many say his great strength was doing the
simple things well which included shot stopping - a telling feature of his game
which enabled The Reds to shore up defence and a establish a solid base upon
which the team as a whole could build. Clemence's arrival was the pivotal ele-
ment in a move to Tranmere Rovers to join old team mate Ron Yeats and his
growing band of former Liverpool players.

Mark Lawrenson

This tall and rangy central defender with great tactical awareness, clean and
effective tackling style, an uncanny ability to read the game and win the ball
from opposition forwards quite possibly formed the greatest defensive pairing
in football history. Not even the greats such as Franz Beckenbauer or Bobby
Moore could have played alongside Alan Hansen and not been pushed into
the shade. Being the Scot's defensive partner must have seemed one of the
most arduous tasks in football. But this Preston born Republic of Ireland

Affectionately known as The Flying Pig Tommy Lawrence was a highly accomplished goalkeeper who saw more than his fair share of glory during his playing days.

international had both the grace and talent to share the limelight.

A club record £900,000 changed hands when he joined from Brighton and Hove Albion. He started out at left back but a string of injuries saw him switch to central defence, then to the left wing and even the heart of midfield when Graeme Souness fell victim to an enforced lay off. His form eventually put paid to Phil Thompson's time at Anfield and set the seal on a trophy laden spell with The Reds.

Before his retirement at the turn of 1988 he had played in every outfield position. An achilles tendon injury suffered in a league game against Wimbledon in March 1987 didn't appear career threatening at the time but just under a year later it accounted for his playing days despite attempts to make a come back.

The League Cup

This competition was viewed as nothing more than an early season distraction for many years. Especially for Liverpool who usually had bigger fish to fry. The Reds didn't even bother to enter during the early seasons. The club's first match came on 19th October 1960. It was a less than convincing 1-1 draw with Luton Town at Anfield. The away leg was a little better as the home side endured a 5-2 trouncing. Southampton knocked Liverpool out in the next round. Until 1978 when The Reds met Nottingham Forest their first final the club had been no further than the fifth round. They had not even competed for the trophy after the Southampton defeat until the 1967-68 season. Wembley played host to the clash with Forest which ended goalless. Liverpool lost the replayed tie at Old Trafford after having a goal disallowed for a very dubious hand ball decision against Terry McDermott. Three years later Liverpool were back. Again the game went to a replay this time at Villa Park. In the first match West Ham had showed plucky resolve and equalised with a late penalty awarded for handling by Terry McDermott. But in the replay The Hammers took an early lead courtesy of Paul Goddard. Kenny Dalglish equalised before Alan Hansen decided the tie.

That win sparked a run of success in the competition as The Reds went on to win the trophy for a further three successive years. Tottenham were beaten 3-1 the following season and Manchester United were edged out 2-1 twelve months after that. Ronnie Whelan was the star of both games. He grabbed two against Spurs and scored the decider against the Old Trafford club with a delightful curved shot from long range. Graeme Souness scored the goal which clinched the trophy in 1984. Everton were beaten 1-0 in a Maine Road replay following the first ever all Merseyside domestic cup final ending in a highly eventful 0-0 draw.

Arsenal were Liverpool's next opponents in the final and despite an early Ian Rush strike The Gunners took the trophy back to Highbury courtesy of two goals from Charlie Nicholas.

Eight years later The Reds were back at Wembley. First Division Bolton Wanderers, a club with a history of slaying giants from the Premier League, proved stiffer opposition than many expected. Steve MacManaman proved to be a worthy man of the match after an afternoon of dazzling wing play and two well taken goals. Alan Thompson tightened the margin of victory with a spectacular volley but he couldn't prevent The Reds becoming the first team to win the trophy five times. In the process Ian Rush became the only player to claim five winner's medals from the competition.

Another Division One outfit Birmingham City faced Liverpool in the first final to be held away from Wembley Stadium. Redevelopment meant the tie was contested at Cardiff's Millennium Stadium. The first domestic cup to be contested outside of England went all the way with a penalty shoot out deciding the outcome. Robbie Fowler's long range volley just before the break looked like it might seal victory for Liverpool but a rash challenge from Stephane Henchoz allowed Birmingham to level just seconds from the end. Extra-time could not separate the two and with the scores level after the first five kicks it was sudden death. Only one more penalty was needed from either side. After Jamie Carragher's successful conversion City's Andrew Johnson saw his shot bounce off Sander Westerveld's arms for a Liverpool victory. The League Cup then known as the Worthington Cup had been the subject of some derision over a number of seasons. Bigger clubs and even a number of smaller outfits were said not to take if seriously preferring to concentrate on League position or other competitions. It was against this backdrop that two of the biggest sides in Europe - Liverpool and Manchester United clashed in the 2003 final. Again the Millennium Stadium played host. The Reds recent form had been desperate while United had eased themselves into championship contention. However, on the day an unfancied Liverpool won a seventh final 2-0 with goals from Stephen Gerrard and Michael Owen late in either half.

League Record

1893	Elected to Division 2
1894-95	Division 1
1895-96	Division 2
1896-1904	Division 1
1904-05	Division 2
1905-54	Division 1
1954-62	Division 2
1962-92	Division 1
1992	FA Premier League

Up until the Premier League's formation Liverpool had won more Football League games than any other club. From the 3524 matches played The Reds had tasted victory in 1650, drawn 851 and lost 1023. They had scored 6071 goals in the process and conceded 4527.

Sammy Lee

Despite standing a mere 5'7" in his stocking feet nobody was ever fooled by his diminished stature, for what he lacked in height he more than made up for in energy and hard headed gumption. The power pack midfielder, a dyed in the wool Liverpudlian, wore his heart on his sleeve. His joy at just playing for Liverpool was only surpassed by his exuberant reaction to victory. A goal on his debut against Leicester City after coming off the bench proved the decider in a 3-2 win. It was a fairy tale start to his dream career which included all of Liverpool's glories through the late 70's and early to mid 80's. In August 1986 he left Anfield when it became clear that he no longer featured in first team plans.

Diminutive midfielder Sammy Lee was a tireless force in Liverpool's successes during the late 1970s and early 1980s. His abilities as a man marker were often utilised against Europe's finest players.

After spells with other English clubs and a stint in Spain he was brought back to Anfield by Graeme Souness in 1991 to coach The Reds' reserve team and now currently coaches the first team.

Tommy Leishman

St Mirren was the stable yard for the young Scotsman who was one of Liverpool's quickest players over short distances. His sudden burst of pace left many defenders struggling to cope. Signed to be a direct replacement for Geoff Twentyman when he was allowed to join Ballymena as player/manager late in

1959. His Anfield career was relatively short lived - limited to just four seasons - until he was superseded by Willie Stevenson. Leishman was nowhere near as good a passer of the ball as his predecessor but what he lacked in finesse, at least in that area of the game, he more than made up for in his appetite for the ball and his ability to win challenges in any area - on the ground or in the air. Despite being a force firmly behind The Reds' successful bid to gain promotion to the top flight he was allowed to leave for Hibernian midway through The Reds' first season back in the top flight when it became clear that his poor distribution was a clear weakness against a better class of opposition. He tried his hand at management after being offered the chance to combine this role with that of player at Linfield of Northern Irish leagues.

Billy Liddell

The very fact that the club was referred to as 'Liddellpool' during his playing

Liverpool stalwart Billy Liddell played 537 games for The Reds and became such a part of the scene at Anfield that many christened the team Liddellpool.

days gives some indication of the esteem in which this Scottish winger was held. He joined the club as a junior just before the war. Liverpool paying his junior side Lochgelly Violets £200 for his services after a tip off about the player from Matt Busby, then a Liverpool player. Other teams were expressing an interest but Liverpool got their man. A consequence of the war was that he had to wait until 1946 until making his first team debut and won a championship medal in his first full season. His first Football League game came against Chelsea in September when Liverpool cruised to a 7-4 win with Liddell scoring twice. The first as early as the third minute.

A bullet like shot from either foot combined with his dribbling skills made him a fearsome opponent and was in no small way responsible for the 229 career goals he scored for The Reds from 537 games. Typically robust and strong he never shirked a tackle or gave up the ball easily, a mark of his consistency being the number of consecutive games in which he managed to play including over 40 in the FA Cup. After 16 seasons at Anfield he retired. Remaining on Merseyside he became Bursar at Liverpool University and a Justice of the Peace. He died in July 2001 aged 79 after a long battle with Alzheimer's Disease.

Alec Lindsay

There is more than just a ground swell of opinion that has Bury born left back Alec Lindsay as the greatest left sided defender England has ever produced. In an age dominated by defenders who defended and did very little else Alec was a rare commodity - a pure footballer. A skill he combined with resolute and earnest defending. Head and shoulders above anything else other sides had to offer it was no surprise when he was handed an England call-up. The note of astonishment being that it was four years into his Anfield career. His arrival in March 1969 at a cost of £67,000 seemed a lot of money for a player who spent the best part of two seasons in the reserves. Most of that time was spent on the left side of midfield where he had come to prominence with his hometown club but after a move to full-back he prospered, teaming up with right full-back Chris Lawler.

While Lawler was always looking to get forward Alec was more likely to ping a ball in to a team-mate's path with his trusty left foot but the result was equally as devastating for the opposition who would be left attempting to defend their lines against a quick attack. With such a solid backline Liverpool came to the fore in the domestic game as well as the European stage. Lindsay never managed to claim the ultimate European prize having been marginalised from the starting eleven after the arrival of Phil Neal. When Neal was switched to right back in place of Lawler Joey Jones essentially ended Lindsay's time on

Merseyside. He moved to Stoke City for a season in the summer of 1977 and then spent the rest of his playing days in the USA with Oakland Timbers of the North American Soccer League.

One of the world famous Liver Birds on its perch alongside the docks. At one time it was said that they would fly away in the event of Liverpool winning the FA Cup. When Liverpool managed to capture the trophy in 1965 after 73 years of trying, they remained in place.

The Liver Bird

This mythical creature has been the central part of Liverpool Football Club's badge for over 100 years and the official symbol of the City of Liverpool since 1797. It is said this is due to the fact that the birds, or at least winged animals which looked rather similar, once inhabited the Mersey Basin area. However, as far as the experts are concerned there is absolutely no evidence that The Liver Bird ever existed.

Other theories as to its true origins of The Liver Bird are that it may be the eagle adopted by King John of England as he chose the once small fishing village of Lerpoole as a base for his campaigns in Ireland during the early part of 13th century. It is also believed that it could have been a Cormorant. When Liverpool was officially created as a Borough the coat of arms included a bird very similar to the Cormorant. In its beak it carried a piece of seaweed. Laver being an old English word for seaweed could have derived the word Liver. It is here that the possibility of an animal which looks like the Liver Bird as we now know it being resident in and around the Mersey becomes most authentic as Cormorants are believed to have nested around the port area in the past. American novelist Herman Melville, who wrote Moby Dick, made mention of the Liver Bird in another novel - Redburn - when he retold the tale of the Liver Bird which he read in a guidebook on a visit to Liverpool in 1839.

The Liver Bird is inextricably linked with the City of Liverpool. Visitors make a point of viewing the two huge statues above the The Liver Buildings on the Pier Head. A sight which for some defines the City's skyline. When Liverpool Football Club was formed clubs had a habit of borrowing the emblem of their town or city to represent their team's crest. As the team bore the same name as the city adopting the Liver Bird it must have seemed the natural choice.

Larry Lloyd

Very few players have left Anfield to enjoy similar or greater heights than they managed to achieve with Liverpool. Larry Lloyd is one player to have bucked the trend. After winning England caps plus UEFA Cup and League Championship winners medals during the 1972-73 season he spent one more year with the club before signing for Coventry City.

The Sky Blues could never scale the heights reached by Liverpool but at the start of The Reds' 1976-77 season he joined Nottingham Forest for £60,000. A bargain buy for Brian Clough. Lloyd was seen as the long term successor to Ron Yeats who was clearly losing the battle to stay in The Reds' line-up due to his advancing years. Larry was built in the same mould as his predecessor. A highly redoubtable yet skilful central defender likely to win all but a minority of aerial battles and to hold his line with great courage and endeavour.

He became a clear first choice by the start of the 1970-71 season and injury allowing remained so until Liverpool grabbed that UEFA Cup and League double. During the season he was an ever present managing 66 games. He would have seemed likely to earn the chance to add an FA Cup win to that honours list but for an ankle injury which ended his run of 27 consecutive games from the start of the season. Reserve teamer Phil Thompson came in to the side and managed to retain his place when Lloyd was fit once more. Missing the chance to play at Wembley was a blow and as Liverpool under new manager Bob Paisley turned to a more stylish manner of defending his days were clearly numbered. £225,000 persuaded The Reds to part company with the man who had cost £50,000 from Bristol Rovers just before the turn of the decade. As a new decade loomed Larry Lloyd proved he still had what it took, claiming not only two European Cup winners medals during his time at The City Ground but league championships too. He also managed to force himself back into the international reckoning once more before seeing out his career with Wigan Athletic, a side he eventually managed before returning to Nottingham to take charge of Notts County.

Ephraim Longworth

To some extent domestic honours passed Ephraim Longworth by even though he won back to back championships with The Reds from 1921-23. Yet he will be remembered as the first Liverpool player to skipper England. Bolton born and bred he spent four years with his local club before arriving at Anfield. The fee was a hefty one but can only be considered as a bargain given the 18 years of loyal service he gave as a player. There were few defenders better at reading the pattern of a game which allowed him to retain his place despite competition from junior pretenders. In the modern game he would be considered a wing back due to his constant probing of the opposition and willingness to start an attack rather than just hoof it clear when the Liverpool were in possession. He became captain of the side not too long after joining - a position he held until 1914. By the time he retired in 1928 he made almost 400 appearances, but for such a forward minded player, surprisingly never managed to find the net.

Joe Louis

The legendary world heavyweight champion of the 1940's would probably have made a more fearsome defender than Alec Lindsay, Neil Ruddock or Tommy Smith, and a far more rugged midfield hardman than Graeme Souness, Steve McMahon or Paul Ince. Despite signing for Liverpool during a promotional tour in 1944 'The Brown Bomber' did not pull on the famous red shirt and test any of the above claims due to his recruitment being nothing more than a publicity stunt for both club and 'player'.

Henry Lowe

A sterling performance against The Reds for Gainsborough Trinity in an FA Cup tie persuaded Liverpool that the defender who preferred to be known as Harry was a prize the club had to have. The game in question was held at Anfield and Liverpool edged through 3-2. Lowe won almost every ball put in his direction and proved to be one of the toughest tacklers the Liverpool forwards had met all season. Within a few months he had joined the club he managed to torment. Injury kept him out of the 1914 FA Cup final with Burnley, a cruel irony considering that he only missed somewhere between four and thirteen games a season. He limped out of the match with Middlesbrough one week before the final and despite constant treatment was ruled out. He began the first Football League season after the war as a Liverpool player but left to join Nottingham Forest in October following just five outings and finding himself second best to Walter Wadsworth.

M

Jason McAteer

There have been few players in the history of the club who can have been more proud to have worn the red shirt of Liverpool than this Birkenhead born Reds fanatic. Football was not the first choice sport for the young Jason McAteer who would eventually attract a £4.5 million transfer fee. Two of his uncles were boxers and the noble art was a serious consideration as a career path. Though once soccer came out on top Jason must have wondered if he should have entered the ring. Pursuit of a club hadn't gone well. Liverpool failed to spot his potential and save themselves many millions of pounds into the bargain. Many more clubs had taken a look but eventually decided to pass up the chance to take him on. After a disastrous trial with Manchester United it is rumoured that the player dumped his boots in the bin. Non-league Marine provided a forum but he struggled at that level to show exactly what he had to offer and mostly turned out for the reserves. Former Liverpool right-back Phil Neal saw something and in 1992 he made his debut for Bolton Wanderers.

The Burnden Park outfit established themselves as promotion hopefuls and cup specialists even knocking Liverpool out at the first hurdle of the FA Cup in January 1993. And at Anfield. The two clubs met once more in the 1995 League Cup final but this time it was Liverpool who came out on top and as a downbeat McAteer trudged away with his loser's medal plans to bring him to Anfield were already a foot. Blackburn Rovers managed by his boyhood hero Kenny Dalglish and Arsenal were keen to do business but when Liverpool threw their hat in the ring there was only going to be one eventual destination. With Bolton and at international level with The Republic of Ireland he had earned rave reviews as a tireless midfielder prepared to run from one end of the pitch to another before delivering a killer ball or shot. That ability to go past players and provide accurate passes was utilised by Roy Evans via the right-back spot. The Liverpool boss was making great use of the wing-back system and McAteer was perfect for the role even if it was just seen as a temporary measure at first in the absence of Rob Jones. The fact that there was always an extra man in the sweeper system to cover during his forays meant the defensive side wasn't as important as it might have been and when Jones returned to full

Born in Kirkby Terry McDermott escaped The Reds' scouting network joining Bury before signing for Newcastle United who he represented in the 1974 FA Cup final against Liverpool.

fitness he was left on the sidelines. A few years later and despite having well over 100 games behind him the love affair between player and club ended in disappointing fashion when with first team chances limited through injury and then the form of others he became one of Brian Kidd's first signings after taking charge of Blackburn Rovers.

John McCartney

A handsome dividend of John Houlding's scouting missions north of the border John McCartney was a member of the first Liverpool squad to kick a ball in earnest having been recruited from Paisley St Mirren. He made little impression during that first season only managing 16 games plus the promotion test match at the end of the campaign. He started the next term as one of the first choice half-backs and proved to be a tough defender to beat as well as a superb passer of the ball once he had it. He, among others, found their talents showcased in the 2nd Division once more after Liverpool were relegated but was a vital member of the side which bounced straight back up after the four match test series proved to be to The Reds liking. He was an ever present during that promotion campaign and missed just three games during the 1897-98 season but still lost his place to Rabbi Howell and never played for the first team again.

Terry McDermott

As Liverpool paraded the FA Cup before their jubilant fans in 1974 Terry McDermott trudged off the pitch with no reason to celebrate the triumph. He wore the black and white stripes of Newcastle. After evading The Reds' scouting system he began his professional career with Bury before moving to St James Park. Six months after that glorious day at Wembley Liverpool brought him back home. Just under a decade later he returned to the North East with a clutch of domestic and European honours as well as the 1980 Professional Footballer's Player of the Year Award. Alongside Kevin Keegan he brought the good times back for The Toon Army. In 1984 he joined Cork City before ending his career with Cypriot side Apoel. The Keegan/McDermott partnership was resurrected along with Newcastle's fortunes in 1992 when he was appointed as a coach. A post he retained when Kenny Dalglish took over the reigns five years later.

Jimmy McDougall

Matt Busby, Tom Bradshaw and Jimmy McDougall formed one of the best defensive partnerships Liverpool have ever been able to field. It was not his original position as he had operated as an inside-forward throughout his early career and when he first joined The Reds. The three never managed to recreate their club partnership for their country as McDougall was the only one capped by Scotland. He also skippered the side in two appearances he made. At club level he spent 10 seasons as an automatic selection only failing to make the side when injury prevented availability. Never a likely goalscorer once he dropped back he contributed eight goals during his first year at Anfield, but only four more more during the remainder of his stay. Mid way through the 1937-38 season and with younger men closing fast in the clamour to make the first team he joined South Liverpool where he spent another season before retiring.

John McKenna

When John Houlding vacated his role at the club following the completion of their inaugural season, Ulster born team manager John McKenna not only stepped into his shoes he filled them more than amply. His family relocated to the city when he was nine. By the time he became involved with Liverpool Football club he was a highly successful businessman.

Although never technically the team manager - the official incumbent was the club secretary W.E. Barclay - it is generally accepted that he was the man who fulfilled most of the tasks the team boss is expected to carry out. His guidance reaped great dividends as the club won the Lancashire League and Football League's Second Division in consecutive seasons. The Reds were relegated after the first campaign in the top flight but it was McKenna's steady hand which ensured they bounced straight back up.

He was a skilled administrator and he held the post of club Chairman twice and had similar responsibilities in the higher echelons of both the Football League and FA. The man working alongside John McKenna throughout his reign, W.E. Barclay stood alongside McKenna and Houlding when the Everton club split in two and the rebellious rump flitted to Goodison Park. His role in taking Liverpool to the pinnacle of the game during the latter part of the 1800's was a substantial one. Player recruitment, scouting and organising the club were his strengths. Along with his loyal sidekick he stepped down for the start of the 1896-97 season but not before he brought a man who he believed could not only take up the mantel but push the club on to bigger and better things - Tom Watson, the manager of Sunderland's team of all the talents.

Donald McKinlay

An incredible 19 seasons at Anfield is a long career by any standards and the fact that the Glasgow born defender managed to maintain his high level of form and fitness for almost two decades demonstrates just what a player he was. Although a redoubtable defender who let all forwards know that they wouldn't pass him without a struggle he perfected the tactic of supporting the attack and managed to score 34 goals. He was comfortable in any berth along the backline and even made appearances in the midfield and on the left-wing. Scotland were quick to offer him caps and with internationals far more prevalent in the modern game there seems no reason why had he been born 80 years later he would not have earned somewhere in the region of 100 appearances for his country rather than the couple he was given - both against home nations. He played 433 games for Liverpool skippering the side during the early 1920s and marshalling his side to successive league titles in 1921-22 and 1922-23. The latter being the only campaign he was an ever present in the side. Injury rather than age was his

Kenny Dalglish's first signing arrived from Aston Villa although he had been a target while still at Goodison park. McMahon's arrival finally seemed to fill the void left by Graeme Souness' departure two years earlier.

enemy when he left Liverpool for local amateur side Prescot Cables. A knock picked up in the last days of the 1927-28 season left him on the sidelines able to make just two appearances throughout the following campaign.

Steve McMahon

A tenacious midfielder who could have joined Liverpool just over two years before he became Kenny Dalglish's first signing as Anfield boss. The Scouser had joined Everton as an apprentice after attending many games as a ball boy.

When he decided to leave Goodison Park it was not for the overtures of The Reds it was to join Aston Villa. He made 75 appearances for the Midlands club before his return to Merseyside. His first goal for The Reds came in a fever pitch Derby game at Goodison Park.

Liverpool had stormed to an early lead thanks to Kenny Dalglish's strike after 20 seconds. Ian Rush doubled the advantage. McMahon grabbed his just before the break to make it 3-0. Though The Reds enjoyed the better of the early exchanges Everton hit back and left Liverpool holding on for the points after a rousing fight back had made it 3-2.

His signing was the catalyst of a new beginning for The Reds who had missed fielding a combative midfield general since Graeme Souness' departure to Sampdoria two years earlier.

Liverpool remained the finest team around and boasted a great midfield but an edge had gone. Macca brought it back. Not to say that his game was just about being a hardman.

He was a far more creative player than most people gave him credit for but it possibly wasn't until the arrival of Barnes, Beardsley, Aldridge and Houghton in the 1987-88 season and the increase in the number of options those players gave him that it became more widely recognised. Liverpool played well almost every game but never more so than when Steve McMahon played well. He produced form that eventually gained him a chance with England in 1988. Alongside Ronnie Whelan the centre-field partnership and dominance of The Reds grew.

Ironically the man who most people think Steve finally replaced was responsible for his departure. Graeme Souness who clearly had other plans for the team allowed him to leave in a £900,000 deal for Manchester City. Two men who played in very similar moulds saw their professional opinions begin to divert. A move was the only option. Again Liverpool were left floundering for inspiration in that area of the field but for many more seasons than had previously been the case. Swindon Town offered McMahon the chance to cut his managerial teeth while still a player after the departure of Glenn Hoddle but cash constraints led to a parting. However, he proved that he still had what it takes to lead players shaping a Blackpool team to promotion via the play-offs yet at one stage of the 2000-01 season they seemed more likely to drop out of the Football League .

Jock McNab

After two years in the reserves Jock McNab forced himself into the Liverpool side which won the title at the close of the 1921-22 season. He was also a key member of the side which retained the championship the following year.

Tough tackling combined with his ability to not only bring the ball forward but use it well made him a valuable asset to The Reds for whom he remained a regular over the next four seasons. Suspension rather than injury being the only reason he ever endured a long lay off. During the 1924-25 season he missed six weeks and 11 games after being sent off in a 1-1 home draw with Newcastle United in February. He made it back for the final game of the campaign but in his absence Liverpool showed indifferent form winning just five games and losing out on a chance to regain the championship, finishing in fourth place. A product of Bellshill Athletic he was capped by Scotland during his time at Anfield. By the time he left the club in 1928 to join Queens Park Rangers he had lost his place to David McMullan and Tom Morrison, after retiring he returned to Merseyside becoming a licensee in Bootle. He played exactly 200 league games before his departure.

Steve McManaman

From his first appearance in a red shirt as a substitute for Peter Beardsley in December 1990 against Sheffield United it was clear that despite his slender frame Liverpool's youth system had unearthed yet another gem via its local network of scouts. His chances were limited by the amount of quality midfielders in The Reds' squad so calls off the bench were his only further taste of action until the 1991-92 season when he was handed a start in the opening game of the season - at home to Oldham Athletic. Four days later he scored his first goal for the club although Liverpool still went down 2-1 away to Manchester City. Injury to key players in the squad had given the 18 year old Scouser and a number of other youngster their chances across the side. McManaman bore the brunt of the extra responsibility making over 50 outings and playing a starring role in the 1992 FA Cup final win over Sunderland.

To some extent that was the best the young Steve McManaman offered Liverpool for many years. Questions about his physical stature, and commitment to the cause were often voiced when things appeared loaded against The Reds. His distribution was also questioned. On his day it was second to none, but his days as far as some were concerned came far too few and far between. These were burdens he was forced to bear until he left The Reds to join Real Madrid on a Bosman transfer in 1999. The theory that he had strung the club along regarding contract talks with his current agreement running out angered many who suggested that once he had signed to play in Spain the following season he should have been dropped from the side.

A couple of years earlier Liverpool had all but sold him to Barcelona. A £12 million deal had been agreed between the clubs in August 1997 but had fallen through with the player's advisors claiming Barca had engineered the deal to attract another player. The fact that he could one day leave the club for nothing formed a position that it was better to receive a huge fee now rather than let him go and realise no profit. Once it became known that the player wasn't afraid to leave but that the club was prepared to let him go speculation surrounded McManaman but he enjoyed possibly his most consistent period for The Reds in the months preceding and following that failed transfer.

From being labelled a promising but unpredictable youngster he had matured into the driving force behind most of Liverpool's attacking moves and had worked so hard on his game that he became not only a great dribbler but one that was virtually impossible to steal the ball away from unless foul play was used. A roving brief allowed him to turn up virtually anywhere on the field and occupy more than just the man marker who was usually deployed to keep him quiet freeing up space for others. Reasons that in no small way upset many when he finally decided to try his luck away from Anfield for a reported £68,000 per week. Despite spells out of Madrid's first team the Liverpudlian played a starring role in his side's comprehensive victory in the 2000 Champions League final nd although he played a more marginal role when Madrid regained the trophy in 2002 it marked a second European Cup win.

The Main Stand
The original design of the Main Stand, built in 1895 and capable of seating 3,000 fans, was bulldozed and replaced by the current structure which was officially opened by the Duke of Kent on 10th March 1973. In the early 80's the Paddock Area was made all seated and as a consequence became the first Anfield stand not to contain terracing.

Managers
The full line of managers since the club's inception is as follows: W E Barclay 1892-1896, Tom Watson 1896-1915, David Ashworth 1920-22, Matt McQueen 1923-28, George Patterson 1928-36, George Kay 1936-51, Don Welsh 1951-56, Phil Taylor 1956-59, Bill Shankly 1959-74, Bob Paisley 1974-83, Joe Fagan 1983-85, Kenny Dalglish 1985-91, Graeme Souness 1991-94, Roy Evans 1994 - 1998*. Gerrard Houllier 1998 - present.

* Gerrard Houllier was appointed alongside Roy Evans as joint manager in July 1998 until Evans left the club in November of the same year.

Manager of the Year Awards
The awards were first held in 1969 and saw Don Revie win three of the first four accolades. Bill Shankly scooped the prize in 1973 following The Reds' first

championship since 1966.

It was the great man's one and only. In the five seasons between 1975 and 1980 Bob Paisley won it four times, and, for another two successive seasons 1981-82 and 1982-83. Joe Fagan made it a hat-trick of Anfield recipients the following year. Kenny Dalglish's first campaign in charge brought him the honour. That was at the completion of the 1985-86 haul. Two seasons later he was voted the league's best boss once more. The legendary Scot was the last Liverpool manager to claim the trophy in 1990 although Gerrard Houllier was widely tipped to scoop the honour after the club's cup treble in 2001. Despite losing out a special merit award was cast by the League Managers' Association to mark the achievement.

Marathon Cup Ties

Competition rules, fixture congestion and police advice have confined the ritual of the marathon FA Cup tie to yesteryear. Liverpool have had their fair share including some of the most exciting the competition has had to offer, especially at the penultimate stage. Amazingly The Reds have won none of them. In 1899 Sheffield United provided tough semi-final opposition. Liverpool held a slender 2-1 lead in the first game at Nottingham but succumbed to an equalising goal which set up a replay at Bolton's Burnden Park. It was a tense affair which ended in a sensational 4-4 draw. A second replay failed to resolve matters when it was abandoned. It was poor luck as Liverpool lead through a George Allan goal. The pitch in Fallowfield Manchester wasn't used for the next game which took place in Derby. Sheffield United went on to contest the final following a 1-0 victory.

In 1962 Bill Shankly entertained his old side, Preston North End, in a 5th round tie. The game finished goalless. A score which was repeated 72 hours later at Deepdale. Not even 30 minutes extra-time managed to separate the sides so it was on to Old Trafford for another replay. The Lancashire club edged past The Reds and no doubt bruised Shanks' pride with a 1-0 win. Six years later and one round further on the road to Wembley West Bromwich Albion were pitted against Liverpool. A 0-0 draw at The Hawthorns led to a return at Anfield.

Tony Hateley provided the lead mid way through the first half but the visitors managed to draw level. Hateley was on target once more in the second replay held at Maine Road but a slender 2-1 scoreline saw The Baggies through to the next stage.

Although not technically a marathon tie the 1979 semi-final with Manchester United was no less exhilarating. It also heralded the first of two titanic cup struggles in successive years.

Maine Road was the neutral venue chosen. Kenny Dalglish put Liverpool ahead after 17 minutes but United not only pegged Liverpool back they managed to seize the advantage. As the minutes ticked away Liverpool's chances of reaching the cup final looked slim. Alan Hansen proved that match saving goals can come from fairly unlikely sources with his 82nd minute strike. The return game at Goodison Park was totally different. Jimmy Greenhoff put United in front early on and despite intense pressure The Reds couldn't find a way through.

Twelve months later Arsenal provided the last four opposition. Which ever team won this tie was a strong favourite to go all the way and lift the cup. Hillsborough saw them fight out a goalless draw. 120 minutes of combat at Villa Park produced a 1-1 scoreline. Almost a fortnight later on the same ground a second replay produced the same result. The only exception being that Liverpool left it very very late. Kenny Dalglish poked the ball home with the last kick of the game. Hopes for a cup win were cruelly dashed in the fourth meeting between the clubs at Highfield Road when the Londoners won 1-0.

League Cup Marathons have been far fewer on the ground. In 1984 Liverpool went on to claim the ultimate prize at Wembley but did so in a very laboured fashion. All but the 2nd round and semi-final ties, which were contested over two legs, needed replays to decide their outcome. Tiny Fulham put up strong resistance taking the League and soon to be European Champions to three games. Craven Cottage was the venue for the original 3rd round encounter which produced no goals. If the West London outfit seemed well pleased to have taken the game to a money spinning Anfield replay the prospect of dragging The Reds back to London for another financially rewarding bite at the cherry combined with the real chance of making that home advantage count must have seemed like manna from heaven. A 1-1 draw after extra time came courtesy of a late penalty to the lower division club made that a reality. However, that tie was decided by a no nonsense Graeme Souness strike four minutes from the end of the additional thirty minutes.

In 1989 Liverpool and Arsenal were the country's top two teams. The third round draw set up a mouth watering clash with the potential to be equally as thrilling as the FA Cup semi-final encounter a decade previously. Anfield hosted a tightly contested 1-1 draw in which John Barnes and David Rocastle scored. The Highbury replay was just as close and finished 0-0. A neutral venue was needed and Villa Park was the natural choice. For the first time in the tie Arsenal held the lead with the only goal of the first half. Steve McMahon equalised just past the hour mark and with extra-time or another replay looming John Aldridge grabbed the winner three minutes from the end.

Marksmen

There can be few clubs able to boast a more impressive array of strikers than Liverpool. Almost from day one there has been a forward at Anfield who is usually a class apart from most of his contemporaries. In the league nine men have hit a century of league goals. Roger Hunt leads the way with 245 followed by Ian Rush (229), Gordon Hodgson (232), Billy Liddell (216), Harry Chambers (135), Jack Parkinson (123), Robbie Fowler (120), Sam Raybould (119), Kenny Dalglish and Dick Forshaw (117). Michael Owen became the last man to join the list in December 2001. His strike at West Ham saw him knock up a century and join Robbie Fowler as the only players to reach this milestone in The Premiership. Jack Balmer was left just one short of the hundred mark in the league but claimed 111 in all competitions. Of those who were also a few strikes short of joining the league centurion club Ian St John (118), John Barnes (106) and Kevin Keegan (100) make the select band in domestic and European cup matches.

Mike Marsh

Though on the surface the Kirkby born midfielder seemed something of a lightweight due to his small stature and wiry build anyone attempting to gain a physical advantage on this basis would come in for a surprise. Mike could mix it with the best of them and packed one hell of a punch but it was as a creative midfielder that his true skills were best suited to the game. When not throwing himself into the tackle he was looking to find an avenue forward and could slit defences as easy as a hot knife melts butter. A substitute appearance in place of Jan Molby back in March 1989 handed him his first slice of senior action. He was called upon from the bench on two more occasions the following campaign. His first start was in the number 7 jersey in the final game of the 1990-91 season. He was to feature far more over the next two years and like many of the youngsters Graeme Souness was forced to press into service due to injury his appearances were sporadic at first. Only during the 1991-92 and 1992-93 seasons did he settle into anything like an automatic selection making 62 appearances in the league scoring just one goal albeit a 30 yard screamer against Crystal Palace in November 1992.

This was one area where his record was criticised. Six strikes from 69 league and cup starts was a low games to goals ratio for a player so fond of coming forward. Clear cut chances were few and far between, although the second goal in the 3-0 home win over Auxerre in the 1991-92 UEFA Cup competition, which tied the aggregate scores and set up a memorable night, will ensure he remains as fondly remembered as any other Liverpool player of his time. An extended run as deputy for Rob Jones at right back curtailed his chances of getting into scoring positions though not his ability to make opportunities for others. The clamour to sign Julian Dicks in September 1993 ended his time on Merseyside as he became one of two Anfield men involved in the players plus cash exchange between Liverpool and West Ham. His value estimated to be around the £1 million mark. A brief stint at Coventry was followed by an even shorter spell at Galatasaray when Graeme Souness was in charge of The Turks. Another Reds midfield stalwart of the 1980s Ronnie Whelan brought him back to The UK with Southend United where he managed to rediscover some of his old form, but a knee injury in 1997 put paid to any chances of him making his way back to the top with Southend or any other club. Forced to retire from the professional game he has played for a number of Conference sides including Kidderminster Harriers whom he helped achieve elevation to the Football League under Jan Molby and Southport then managed by another former Liverpool player Mark Wright.

Match Fixing

It may seem hard to believe that any Liverpool player would want to lose to Manchester United but that's what four Liverpool players were found guilty of in 1915. Rumours that the football league was about to suspend the professional game due to the advent of the First World War were abound. Nobody knew exactly how long the conflict would last. Players were rightly worried that it would end their careers. Some knew it would as no matter if the war lasted six months or six years their playing days were over.

The temptation to make as much money as they could before it happened proved too much for some. Liverpool were safe in mid-table mediocrity while United were languishing far too close to the foot of the table for comfort. If United claimed the points it could only aid their fight against relegation and of course if the result of a game was already decided before a ball was kicked there was the chance for those in the know to make an awful lot of money by well placed betting.

United had seven to one odds to win 2-0. The game played on Good Friday at Old Trafford brought nothing but suspicion upon itself. George Anderson put United ahead and was expected to double the advantage when a penalty was awarded in the home side's favour. He was the club's regular penalty taker and had a good record from the spot.

However, Patrick O'Connell took responsibility and blazed his shot well wide. Suspicious enough. But when Liverpool striker Fred Pagnam hit the bar he was openly remonstrated for his effort. Anderson grabbed a second late into the game to make the final score 2-0. Bookmakers decided that a fix had been arranged and publicly offered a reward for information leading to the identification of those involved in the planning. An inquiry was set up and after lengthy consideration decided that a betting coup had taken place. Four players from each club were held to be the culprits and immediately banned for life although their sentence was removed after the war as a reward for their sterling service in name of king and country. As a former United player Jackie Sheldon was thought to be heavily influential. The other Anfield players named were Tommy Miller, Bob Purcell and Tom Fairfoul. The club itself was fined £250. The latter offender never returned to Liverpool. Sheldon and Miller went on to make many more appearances for the club. When he eventually left Anfield Miller actually joined United.

Dominic Matteo

Anyone regularly turning up for Liverpool reserve games during the early '90s couldn't help but admire the talents of a young man who seemed able to play equally well in any position. Often his outings for the second string would be as a centre-back but during starts in either this position or on the left for the first team he looked comfortable. He had been spotted by Kenny Dalglish playing for a youth side in Southport. The Liverpool boss had originally gone to see his son Paul play and while not looking to add new talent to his squad ended up paying more attention to Dominic than Dalglish junior. An offer of terms at Anfield was accepted by the Scottish born youngster but his debut was handed out by Graeme Souness. For those with little knowledge of Matteo any nerves about fielding him at the highest level were quickly dispelled as he proved himself to be not only a sturdy defender when pressed but a forward going player both comfortable on the ball and in his use of it.

His outings still tended to be piecemeal and as an alternative when injury or suspension hit others until the 1997-98 campaign when he finally appeared to be making and retaining the rewards so richly deserved. The recruitment of others in his position most notably Sami Hyppia and Stephane Henchoz by Gerrard Houllier did affect his chances of continuing to be a force and a £4 million plus transfer to Leeds United during the late summer of 2000 provided the opportunity to show just what else he was capable of.

Jimmy Melia

During the 1980s the former Reds forward would haunt his former club pulling off crucial victories as manager of Brighton and Hove Albion. One of the most notable being to knock Liverpool out of the 1982-83 FA Cup on the way to taking his unfancied side all the way to Wembley in a win that was achieved at Anfield. A local lad he was recruited on to the groundstaff at 15 and by the end of 1955 was inducted into the first team squad managing to score a goal on his debut against Nottingham Forest. He was not only a player who could notch goals he was also a schemer who could set up chances for others. The 1958-59 season was his most prolific as a goalscorer when 21 efforts converted in 39 games made him the club's top scorer. That was a role he lost to Roger Hunt over the remainder of his time with Liverpool but he still weighed in with a respectable tally and in four of his eight full seasons with the club managed to reach double figures in the league.

The 1961-62 promotion campaign was by far his most consistent and one in which he remained an ever present. He missed just three games in his first season in the top flight but found goals far harder to come by despite continuing to work as hard as ever at his passing and overall contribution to the team. Although full of running and literally willing to give his all in the Liverpool cause he was surpassed by a younger generation of hopefuls and allowed to join Wolves in March 1964. His stay was short lived and his first taste of football on the South Coast began with Southampton just over a season later. He saw out his playing days with Aldershot and Crewe Alexandra also managing both sides while still playing.

He retired in 1972 to become full time manager at Gresty Road before heading home to take charge of troubled Southport for a short spell in 1975. He spent a number of years outside the professional game before returning with Brighton. Two years with Belenenses of Portugal followed. Stockport County provided his next and last appointment in English club management in 1986.

Melwood

The Reds' training ground was constructed many years before it received a major revamp during the early 60s. Billy Shankly deemed the facilities to be nothing less than appalling on his arrival at the club and made their upgrading a priority. Since which time Melwood has been at the forefront of both medical and physical technology.

Men of the Cloth

James Jackson was not your average footballer. His determination to follow a religious career was well known. While still playing he became a church Elder and after studying for a degree in Philosophy and Greek he undertook the necessary theology course for him to become a Reverend. The Liverpool fans had called him 'the Parson' for many years. He finally retired from the game in 1933 at which time he was ordained. In 1947 he conducted the funeral of a former club Chairman, W.H. O'Connell.

Signed from Aberdeen in the latter months of 1925 in just under three years he was appointed club captain. His father was also a professional footballer who made many appearances for Glasgow Rangers, Newcastle United, West

Ham and Arsenal. Though a talented right back he also turned out across the defence and midfield - on both flanks. The only area he didn't seem to excel in was goal scoring. He managed two strikes in 224 appearances.

Mercantile Credit Centenary Tournament

When the Football League celebrated its centenary season in 1987-88 they organised a tournament for the 16 teams with the most consistent records over the first part of the campaign. They would fight it out over a weekend mini tournament sponsored by Mercantile Credit. The qualifiers were split into two pools then drawn against each other in cup fashion. Liverpool were in the first phase along with Blackburn Rovers, Aston Villa, Leeds United, Nottingham Forest, Newcastle United, Wimbledon and Tranmere Rovers. A vastly shortened game of twenty minutes each way would be settled by sudden death penalties should the scores be level. Most were including The Reds' first and only tie. Newcastle triumphed 1-0 courtesy of Mirhandinha. The line up showed Liverpool had no intention of taking the event seriously.

Tom Miller

A Motherwell born striker who had enjoyed spells and scored a number of goals with Larkhill Hearts, Gleniven, Lanark United, Third Lanark and Hamilton Academical before turning up at Anfield towards the end of the 1911-12 season. He made his debut days after joining Liverpool and managed to play in eight of the final 13 games of the league season scoring in his third game. A 1-1 draw with Middlesbrough. The Reds finished 17th in a very ordinary season and with 49 goals scored throughout the league campaign were in clear need of extra fire power. Miller provided this with 52 goals from the 127 games he played for the club in various attacking capacities. As he was able to lead the line and also able to support other forwards when called upon. Many players were capable of switching in this way but few could do it with such devastating effect. He played in the 1914 FA Cup final but was far from the Tom Miller Liverpool fans had come to expect.

Just under a year later with the Football League set to suspend competition and thereby the professional game and the players' earning potential Miller was one of the players caught fixing a result in a game with Manchester United in order to capitalise on a betting coup. Though originally banned for life as a punishment he saw this penalty overturned after the war and after just over a season with The Reds he ironically joined the Old Trafford club.

Gordon Milne

Gordon Milne arrived in August 1960 for £16,000. A club record fee was

Few players had the skills, vision and passing ability of Jan Molby, who was signed from Ajax in 1984.
He left Anfield in February 1996 after well over a decade with the club.

required when Bill Shankly went back to his former club Preston to recruit one of his earliest transfers.

Gordon was the son of his former partner on North End's wing Jimmy Milne. The young man established a dynamic link with Ronnie Yeats and Alec Leishman. All three men read the game well. Anticipation of the opposition's ideas and accurate passing were his individual strengths. He wasn't afraid to come forward either and could usually be found supporting the attack his intuitive play initiated.

Both his career lows came within the space of a year. A knee ligament injury meant he missed the 1965 cup final win. When he regained full fitness for the following campaign he was in scintillating form and made 14 appearances for England in the months preceding the 1966 World Cup Finals but he didn't make the shake up for a squad place.

Tommy Smith's arrival on the scene was a major factor in his £30,000 move to Blackpool in the summer of 1967. After retiring he established a very successful career as a manager.

Jan Molby

Almost as soon as he arrived some observers were writing the Danish midfielder off as nothing more than a luxury player able to offer little more than the occasional appearance where he stroked the ball around well but ultimately flattered to deceive on all other occasions. The end result was that he was in and out of the side during his first season managing 19 starts and three appearances from the bench. The following season was a totally different story. He missed just three games in Kenny Dalglish's first season securing League Championship and FA Cup winners' medals by the end of the campaign. Molby's role in the Wembley win was vital. Liverpool had their backs to the wall for most of the game but came out of the shadows thanks to the Dane taking hold of the game and finally managing to begin sustained periods of pressure. Everton crumbled when he supplied the killer ball for Ian Rush's equaliser and had virtually no answer to the virtuoso display orchestrated by Jan which brought two more goals.

In truth this is exactly the type of display he had been turning in most of the season and which had guided Liverpool to a title that looked destined to belong anywhere but Anfield at the turn of the year. That was until The Reds dropped just seven points from a possible 54. He maintained his form the following season though Liverpool as a team did not.

Injury limited his appearances over the next 12 months as he wore a shirt number other than 12 or 14 just once. A stint in prison for driving offences during the 1988-89 campaign gave him the opportunity to add just 12 more appearances to his tally. Almost all of which were as a makeshift partner for Alan Hansen in the centre of defence. Rather than sack their employee Liverpool and Kenny Dalglish stuck by their player after his release from gaol assuring him that if he would be treated no differently from the other players in the squad with starting places being judged on playing merit and no other criteria.

He remained at Anfield until February 1996 when he took up a post as player/manager of Swansea City although just before this had spells on loan with Barnsley and Norwich City. Other players had forced their way into the picture and, with the skills that had put him head and shoulders above any other midfielder in the country being shown only fleetingly over his final few seasons at Anfield, he ended a over decade of service with almost 300 appearances under his belt and 58 goals many of which were from dead ball situations.

John Molineux

In 1955 John Molineux was a player signed as a cure to a lean looking defence. He took over the troubled right back spot from Ray Lambert and formed a steady partnership with Ronnie Moran. Liverpool conceded 33 less goals over the 1955-56 season than they had the previous campaign. Though 63 compared to 96 in the goals against column was progress it was still far too many if The Reds were to go up without a struggle. A more defensively minded player than many of his recent predecessors he was as strong in the tackle as any other player in the division. Despite playing just three league games in the 1961-62 season he contributed to Liverpool finally being promoted to the top flight. The movement of Dick White to right full-back was ultimately responsible for Molineux losing his place and he rejoined the club that had sold him to Liverpool - Chester for £2,000. The club on the English/Welsh border realised a £1,500 profit on the two deals. He played on until 1965 when he joined New Brighton.

The Moores Family

For as many years as anyone can remember a member of the Moores' family, founders of the Littlewoods Shopping empire, have held some kind of interest in one or both of the city's clubs. Merseyside soccer has found the family great benefactors. Their controlling share of Everton was bought in the early 1990's by Peter Johnson the former chairman of Tranmere Rovers. However, Liverpool still have a family member at the helm. David Moores the current club Chairman and boyhood Kopite is the founding father John Moore's grandson and took on the role in August 1991.

Ronnie Moran

An Anfield stalwart both on and off the pitch Ronnie Moran was recommended by a postman on his daily round to one of the Liverpool directors. Joining the club in 1952 as a 17 year old he went on to serve as player, coach, assistant manager and eventually caretaker boss. His playing days proved to be distinguished if somewhat injury prone. He enjoyed fairly consistent seasons from 1955-56 until he became a first choice selection for the 1959-60 campaign. In the five seasons which followed he made 127 appearances compared to the 218 League and cup games he featured in the five seasons previously. Over time Gerry Byrne forced him out of the reckoning. An invitation to join Bill Shankly's back room team once his playing days were over in 1965 proved too good to resist. He remained a vital member of The Boot Room until the end of the 1997-98 term when he retired aged 64.

He managed the team for the weeks between Kenny Dalglish's resignation and Graeme Souness' appointment in 1991. When Souness underwent heart bypass surgery prior to the 1992 FA Cup Final he stepped into the hot seat once more. The honour of leading the team out against the losing finalists Sunderland was extended to him. It was a worthy accolade to a modest man.

Tom Morrison

An Ayrshire born right-half who won honours both before and after joining The Reds with St Mirren - the Scottish FA Cup and Sunderland - the league championship. Liverpool had recruited him at a cost of £4,000 in January 1928 and after 254 career games he was allowed to leave for Roker Park. There were no medals for all his endeavours at Anfield only the reward of a job well done. A sturdy tackler when called upon to defend he was also a creative player who could release killer balls over any distance. Jobs he did well over the six full seasons he enjoyed at Anfield. With Sunderland he was encouraged to drop back on to the right hand side of defence, a position in which he excelled. A strange fact uncovered about the player is that during the 1936-37 season he was playing under an assumed name for a youth side in Cambridgeshire.

N

Phil Neal

In October 1974 Northampton's promising right back became Bob Paisley's first signing. Despite those humble beginnings he finished up as English football's most decorated player claiming a record eight championship medals to go with four European Cups and the same number of League Cup winners' medals. Just for good measure there were UEFA and Super Cup wins to go with them. He is the only Liverpool player to have appeared in all five of the club's European Cup finals and became club captain in 1984 following Graeme Souness' departure for Sampdoria. But in one of the game's strangest twists of fate the club's most successful player never got to lift a trophy as skipper. As skipper Kenny Dalglish gave the arm band to Alan Hansen shortly after his appointment as manager. There was some suggestion that Phil himself had been offered the post when Joe Fagan announced his retirement but whatever the rights and wrongs of that claim he didn't have to wait too long for an offer to further his managerial ambitions.

In December 1985 he was appointed player/manager of Bolton Wanderers and took the club to the old 2nd Division though narrowly failed in his bid to get them back into the top flight despite reaching the play-off finals. Further posts at club and international level have followed.

Steve Nicol

Steve Nicol began his Anfield career as a left back but he was switched between the two flanks countless times and very often asked to play in the centre of defence during his first few seasons. Liverpool boss Bob Paisley saw him principally as a right-back but understudying Phil Neal was no easy route into the first XI. His chance to really secure a place in the side was in midfield as a replacement for the injured Craig Johnston in October 1983. So impressive was his form that he remained in the side once the Aussie born winger was fit and earned a championship medal. He was a member of the side that secured a fourth European Cup win after the dramatic penalty shoot-out in Rome's Olympic Stadium, bravely volunteering to take the first kick which he lofted high over the bar.

Scottish international Steve Nicol was a willing volunteer to take a penalty in the 1984 European Cup final shoot out. He missed but Liverpool went on to win the trophy.

After ousting Sammy Lee from the side he finally succeeded to the right-back spot after Phil Neal left to become player/manager of Bolton Wanderers. His attacking flair was evident in every position he played including defence. At full-back he regularly overlapped to create an extra attacking option and more often than many other defenders found himself on the end of a move with 45 goals from his 437 starts. Many Liverpool fans still fondly recall his scoring spree during the early part of the 1987-88 season when, in conjunction with John Barnes, he tore defences apart and bagged six goals in as many games, including a well taken hat-trick against Newcastle United before a live TV audience. Before leaving The Reds in January 1995 he won every honour in the game bar the League Cup. A free transfer to Notts County to take up coaching responsibilities alongside his playing duties under former Everton boss Howard Kendall was bitter sweet ending just over a season later. He returned to the top flight with Sheffield Wednesday for two seasons before securing a lucrative deal to play and coach in the North American Soccer League.

Berry Nieuwenhuys

Difficulty in mastering the exact pronunciation of his surname led to the South African simply being referred to as 'Nivvy'. He joined the club in 1933 and made 260 appearances in nine seasons scoring 79 goals.

His distinguished career was slightly tarnished during the war when he wrote to a club he was due to guest for. The gist of his letter was to request terms in excess of the £2 per game fee payable to professionals. It was common practice to pay more, however it was the Springbok's bad luck that he was caught red handed. A lifetime ban issued as punishment was revoked soon after the hostilities ended due to his service in the conflict. He extended his time at Liverpool, playing his last game in 1947. It was his fifteenth of the season which qualified Berry for a championship medal.

Nicknames

Liverpool's officially recognised nicknames are The Reds or Pool.

The Number 7 Shirt

Many great Liverpool players have worn various shirt numbers but the man in the number 7 jersey always seems to have enjoyed a unique position with the club and the adulation of the fans. When shirts were first numbered it was customary for the outside right to wear it. This included wing aces like Jack Cox, Bill Lacey, Arthur Goddard, Jackie Sheldon, Jimmy Payne and Berry Nieuwenhuys.

Ian Callaghan claimed the hallowed number on his debut and never really let go of it until Kevin Keegan's arrival 11 years later. Kenny Dalglish inherited the honour following Keegan's departure for Germany and took the reputation of the Liverpool number 7 to heights even his predecessor hadn't scaled. As Kenny gently eased himself upstairs and off the playing field a few others tried the shirt on for size but the next memorable custodian was Peter Beardsley, a man more than capable of carrying the torch he'd been given. Dean Saunders was next in line then Nigel Clough who was the first player to hold the number under the new squad system. When Clough left Anfield it was the turn of another dazzling crowd pleaser Steve McManaman to take over the mantel, which he did with great effect until his transfer to Real Madrid in the summer of 1999. Czech international Vladimir Smicer took the number for the start of the next campaign retaining it until the signing of Australian international Harry Kewell from Leeds United in 2003.

O

One match one goal wonders

To date only a couple of players have scored in their first and only appearance for Liverpool. B. Bull scored in the 6-1 home thrashing of Lincoln City in January 1896 and John Sealey who grabbed a goal just before half time in the final game of the 1964-65 season when Liverpool beat Wolves 3-1 at Molineux.

The One Up Club

Despite hundreds, in some cases many hundreds of appearances for The Reds some players have just one goal to show for all their efforts in the Liverpool cause. Scoring certainly isn't the best way to gauge a player's contribution to the club but still makes very interesting reading.

Among the most notable members of this select club are Laurie Hughes a veteran of 326 games who struck an 88th minute equaliser against Preston North End. Gary Ablett notched in his second game for the club and Anfield debut. Howard Gayle grabbed one in a 1-1 draw with Spurs not long after his heroic 1981 European Cup semi-final display against Bayern Munich and in the process scored Liverpool's first goal in around 270 minutes of league football.

Dick White spared the blushes in the 3rd round of the 1958 FA Cup tie with Southend United when he levelled the game averting a very embarrassing exit from the competition and setting up an Anfield replay which The Reds won 3-2. Bobby Campbell was a loyal servant of eight seasons but he too had just one goal to boast of when his Liverpool career ended.

The full list of one up club members who have played 50 games or more follows:

Laurie Hughes 326 Dick White 216 Phil Babb 164 Archie Goldie 150 Gary Ablett 144 Roy Saunders 144 Matthew McQueen 87 David Pratt 85 John McConnell 53 Nicky Tanner 48(5)

Opening Day of the Season

Liverpool have opened campaigns with more wins than any other first class club. When The Reds beat Aston Villa in the first game of the 2002-03 season

Although he came to the attention of a global audience during the 1998 World Cup Liverpool fans had been singing the praises of Michael Owen since he made his first team debut just over a year earlier.
Introduced as a substitute the then 17 year old scored within minutes of coming off the bench.

it meant that in 99 league seasons Liverpool had claimed victory on 60 occasions.

Ronald Orr

Ronald Orr went on a prodigious scoring spree just weeks after joining the club from Newcastle United in April 1908, netting five times from the seven games he played. The following season he was top scorer by some distance claiming 20 of the 57 league goals Liverpool scored and bagged three from two FA Cup games. He never reached those dizzy heights again and over the next two seasons scored nine times. Two of those strikes came in a thrilling 6-5 win over his former club. Liverpool trailed 5-2 at half-time but turned in a magnificent performance in the second half. The signing of Tom Miller proved to be the factor which hastened his departure in April 1912, after just seven outings he returned to his native Scotland to join Raith Rovers but came south of Hadrian's Wall once more to play for South Shields before retiring.

Michael Owen

Perhaps the most famous product of Liverpool's youth system burst on the scene towards the end of the 1996/97 season. He grabbed a debut goal in an away draw with Wimbledon.

A week later he was given his first start when Liverpool travelled to Sheffield Wednesday and retained his place in the side for the opening game of the 1997/98 campaign. With Robbie Fowler nursing a serious injury the youngster was paired with the experienced Karl Heinz Riedle - a European Cup winner. In the Coca-Cola Cup tie against Grimsby during the opening weeks of the season he scored his first hat-trick.

Despite the usual caution displayed by managers when introducing youngsters to the first team his place in the side was a cast iron certainty as is a spot in the England set up. Already acclaimed as one of the finest strikers in the world Michael will remain a key member of any squad. His stature outside the game is also sky high following his displays in the 1998 World Cup in France and the dignified way he handled the many bouquets thrown his way. Like his club Owen enjoyed a moderate season following his exploits in France. A crop of injuries limited the number of appearances he was able to make but by the close of the 2000-01 season he was firing on all cylinders scoring both goals in the 2-1 FA Cup Final win over Arsenal. In each of his six seasons as a first team regular at Anfield he has finished as top scorer.

Own Goals

Putting through your own net is an occupational hazard for any player. However, as the pundits say these things probably average themselves out over the course of a season. Some of the most notable own goals in matches involving Liverpool include two scored in the 1985-86 Littlewoods Cup semi-final second leg with Queens Park Rangers. The Londoners took the opening game by a single goal at Loftus Road. With The Reds flying high in both the League and FA Cup there was little doubt about their ability to overturn the deficit and secure a place in the final. Especially when Steve McMahon opened the scoring minutes before half time. Rangers equalised with an Alan Hansen own goal and held the advantage once more. Craig Johnston levelled the tie with a little over half an hour remaining. Extra time looked a certainty until an attempted clearance three minutes from time rebounded off Gary Gillespie's backside and bobbled past the despairing defenders.

P

Bob Paisley

How do you follow a man like Bill Shankly? The Scot had set out on a mission to make Liverpool the best team not just in the land, not even in Europe, but in the world. As he termed it: "A bastion of invincibility". At the time Shanks took over he decided to leave the men that comprised the back room staff in post. When he called it a day in July 1974 there were plenty of suggestions as to who his successor should be. Some thought it should be a tried and tested manger who could take the team that last extra couple of inches or so. Brian Clough and Don Revie were mentioned in dispatches as were former Anfield players such as Ian St John and Ronnie Yeats. However, the opinion of the Liverpool board was the only one that counted. They shared Bill's confidence in his seconds and saw Bob as the man to fill the void. He never actually wanted the job and couldn't see himself as a manager only agreeing to take it after much persuasion. It was accepted on the understanding that it would be on a short term basis until a younger, more suited, man could be found. It later emerged that the reluctant deputy had spent the best part of a month trying to make Shanks reverse his decision.

Bob was the epitome of the one club man. After joining Liverpool in 1939 as a 19 year old from Bishop Auckland he spent the rest of his working life and some time beyond that at Anfield. Just prior to his arrival he had won the FA Amateur Cup. He was technically a Liverpool player at the time but was given special permission by the club to appear in the final.

His peak years were probably taken by the war but a distinct highlight was a medal for his part in the 1946-47 championship winning campaign. Missing out on selection for the 1950 FA Cup Final despite scoring the first goal in the semi-final win over Everton was something he never really got over and when he had to leave a player out of his line up he could honestly say he knew how it felt.

A career beyond his playing days had already been prepared. He achieved a physiotherapy qualification via a correspondence course. This provided an insight which was to serve the club and its players well. It was said that he could diagnose an injury simply by watching a player, which saved much

The Paisley Gateway erected in honour of the former Liverpool manager Bob Paisley sits in the shadow of the new Kop Grandstand.

unnecessary suffering and meant treatment could be given earlier thus reducing absences from the action. Various board members felt he still had plenty to offer the club on the coaching side so in 1954 an offer was made and accepted. Bob's first job was to manage the reserves.

His third season at the helm led to the club's first ever Central League title. On Bill Shankly's arrival he switched to first team trainer and on his departure became manager. Upon calling it a day in 1983 he was the most successful manager in the history of English football with an amazing 15 trophies and six Manager of the Year awards secured in just nine years.

The completion of an unprecedented third League Cup win on the trot led to a touching display of affection by his players as they ushered him up the famous steps to collect the trophy. It was a gesture which summed up his relationship with them - something akin to a favourite uncle and mentor who deserved a piece of the limelight for all the hard work behind the scenes.

Already a director Bob was asked to fulfil an advisory role to Kenny Dalglish when the Scot was made manager in 1985. In January 1992, the beginning of the club's centenary year, he became a Vice-president of Liverpool Football Club. It was to be the last post he held at Anfield.

It seems a tragedy that the shrewd and acutely tactical brain that had brought so much glory to Liverpool and pride for its supporters was in the end taken from him by Alzheimer's Disease. If the touching tributes left at the ground were any indication every fan in the country and beyond mourned his passing on February 14th 1996. He was a great man who earned respect from everyone.

Jack Parkinson

Signed as an amateur in 1899 the Bootle born forward was restricted to just one outing over the next four years as he tried in vain to unseat Sam Raybould. An injury to the master allowed his apprentice to feature 18 times during the 1903-04 season. Once Raybould was fit Parkinson was forced out once more. It became clear that something had to give if he was to have any chance of staking a claim to a starting berth and tactically it was a master stroke which saw him move to inside left where he provided a link between midfield and the two main strikers. On the back of this Liverpool claimed the 2nd Division title with some distance to spare with Parkinson notching 20 goals. In one of the cruellest twists of fate even suffered by this player he missed out on the chance to play a full part in the title winning season which followed after breaking his wrist in the opening game of the season against Woolwich Arsenal only returning for eight of the final nine games of the campaign. He showed the lay off had caused him to lose none of his sharpness scoring after just five minutes of his return and hitting another six by the final game.

He remained on the fringes until the 1909-10 season although still hit a goal almost every game from the 34 appearances he made over the next three seasons. When given the chance of an extended run he scored 30 goals from 31 games to finish as top scorer and by the time he ended his fifteen year association with Liverpool Football Club had claimed 128 goals from a total of 222 games. A feat which made him the club's highest ever goalscorer - he edged out old rival Sam Raybould by a single strike and ensured he remained in the club's top 10 goalscorers until the turn of the following century.

Maurice Parry

A Welsh born player who enjoyed a long career throughout the United Kingdom and Europe. He joined Liverpool in 1900 and played all but a couple of his 221 career games as a right-half. There were few better in the business and as a strong ball winner who could use possession effectively once he had it he proved to be a star turn in the eight seasons he was at Anfield. He played a vital role in The Reds' promotion as 2nd Division champions and then claiming the title in successive seasons from 1904-05 to 1905-06. After gaining over 200 appearances for The Reds and 16 caps for his country while at Anfield, he moved on to Partick Thistle. On retiring he managed Rotherham County then coached Barcelona, Eintracht Frankfurt and Cologne.

Jimmy Payne

For a time Jimmy Payne was compared to some of the great wingers produced by the English game. A contemporary of Stanley Matthews and Tom Finney had to have something to be talked about in the same breath as these names and many others. He made his debut in the 1948-49 season and remained a first choice selection for five seasons. A move towards the centre of the field ended both his status as an Anfield regular and his time with Liverpool. A modern day comparison to his body structure would be that of Steve McManaman. Fine for flying down the wing and delivering balls inside but not too well designed for the demands of becoming a more central midfielder. His body let alone his heart just wasn't up to the tasks demanded of it. Injuries blighted his last three seasons at the club and when they weren't keeping him out his form could. No longer able to peel defences in the manner he once did Payne decided moving to Everton was a step forward. But things went from bad to worse and after six outings towards the end of the 1955-56 season he retired from the professional game and still the right side of 30. What he may have had to offer The Reds and England had it not been for his setbacks remains a mystery but any one who ever saw him in his hey day run past player after player will testify that Jimmy Payne could have achieved so much more.

Penalties

Over the years Liverpool have had many great penalty takers able to keep their cool and grasp the advantage a spot kick brings. None were more fearsome to the facing goalkeeper than Phil Neal. When he took over the responsibility from Kevin Keegan at the end of 1975 he capped the event by scoring two penalties in a 2-2 home draw with Arsenal. By far his most famous spot-kick would be the one to make the 1977 European Cup Final safe. Though a frequent scorer from the spot it would be unfair to assume that most of his 60 career goals for The Reds came from the dead ball. He was equally as dangerous from open play. Jan Molby was a worthy successor to his mantel. The Dane's laid back style of play may have made him the natural choice; when the heat was on he could always keep his cool. While snaps of any crucial cup final penalties may not grace the Molby family album he did bear the responsibility for many game saving or winning spot kicks. The quarter final cup tie with Watford in the 1985-86 Cup winning trail springs to mind. Just months later he recorded the rare feat of scoring a hat-trick of penalties in a League Cup 4th Round replay win over Coventry City. It earned him a unique place in the Anfield history books.

A run of injuries and off the field problems limited Molby's appearances, and in his absence John Aldridge assumed the duty. The burden would usually pass back if Jan was on the field but the amiable striker showed he had enough right to take over. By the end of his first full season at Anfield - the record breaking 1987-88 campaign - he had converted all ten of the spot kicks awarded to him. The eleventh and most vital came in the FA Cup Final as a direct result of a tackle on Aldo himself. Wimbledon led 1-0 with around thirty minutes remaining. The striker found himself with the ball at his feet and in the territory he knew best, the penalty area. With his back to the goal he tried to make some space and turn around. The Reds were in the ascendancy and at that stage of the game lay constant siege to Dave Beasant's goal. Should the newly crowned league champions grab one at that moment they would be clear favourites to go on and win the match, the cup and a then unprecedented double double. The award was controversial and to this day the Wimbledon players still argue that Clive Goodyear's challenge should never have been penalised. Even the match referee admits that with the benefit of hindsight and a different angle he would not have given the decision.

At the time none of this was going through John's mind as he prepared to grab the vital lifeline he had been given. He struck the ball firmly and low to the right. Only to see the giant keeper follow its course then palm it to safety. As a result Aldridge became the first player to miss a penalty in the cup final.

The Reds have won trophies in matches decided by penalties. By far the most renowned being the 1984 European Cup Final victory. 90 minutes and then extra time failed to separate Liverpool and Italian side AS Roma who were level at 1-1. When the referee blew to indicate he was ready for the sides to settle the tie from 12 yards out almost everyone in Rome's Olympic Stadium (Roma's home ground) was surprised to see Steve Nicol step forward to take the first. He spooned it hopelessly over the bar. The Italians made no mistake with their first leaving Liverpool's hopes on a knife edge. Phil Neal eased things a little by converting the second. Then the highly experienced Bruno Conti put his effort high and wide. It remained level until the penultimate round of kicks as Souness, Righetti and Rush made no mistake with their chances. Bruce Grobbelaar with nothing to lose in this situation seemed to employ as many tactics as he could think of to put the visibly nervous Graziani off. The Italian had already placed the ball on the spot as a lethargic Grobbelaar slowly looped towards goal. Once there the South African went for a little wander around before setting on his line and using his now infamous spaghetti legs technique. He looked as weak as a kitten when his knees seemed to give way and his legs wobbled.

When the penalty was eventually taken it too ended up in the crowd. That meant that Alan Kennedy had to convert his effort. He did and to the ecstatic congratulations of his colleagues and the massed ranks of Liverpool fans lucky enough to be there.

That European Cup success wasn't The Reds' first silverware from a shoot out. The 1974 Charity Shield came to Anfield as Liverpool beat Leeds United 6-5 on penalties. The game had finished 1-1 over ninety minutes.

Other than finals Liverpool's most important victory from the ultimate tie breaker was the 1992 FA Cup semi-final replay. Portsmouth had almost put The Reds out of the competition in the first game staged at Highbury. Ronnie Whelan's strike from close range saved his team and set up a return game at Villa Park which also ended in a draw. Not even extra-time could break the stalemate. One replay was allowed and the rules said that penalties would decide who would go on to meet Sunderland at Wembley. Anfield's only FA Cup shoot-out came in January 1995. Birmingham City had held the home side to a 1-1 draw. Another 30 minutes saw very few chances on goal as both sides proved cautious. Liverpool took the tie 2-0 on penalties.

The same opposition were The Reds' victims in the 2001 Worthington Cup final when Liverpool became the first side to win a domestic cup through this route. With the scores tied at 1-1 after extra-time and replays no longer held by the Football League penalties were the method used to settle the destination of the trophy. Liverpool seized an early advantage scoring each of their first three spot-kicks while Birmingham missed their first. Dietmar Hamman saw his effort rebound back off the keeper resulting in sudden death. Andrew Johnson's miss following Jamie Carragher's successful strike secured the game and the cup. At the end of 5th paragraph insert: In the early rounds of the 2002-03 competition Ipswich Town were beaten at Anfield as The Reds made their way to another successful run to Cardiff.

Anfield's list of regular penalty takers includes Billy Liddell, Don McKinlay, Gordon Hodgson, Ronnie Moran, Jack Balmer and Tommy Smith.

During the 1954-55 season ten penalties were awarded against Liverpool in just eight games. Nine were successfully converted including two in the same game from Cyril Done then of Port Vale but a former Liverpool player. Vale ran out 4-3 winners as a result. The season before Liverpool had been effectively consigned to relegation by Cardiff City when Alf Sherwood had to go in goal for regular keeper Ron Howells who had been injured. He faced Billy Liddell who had a fearsome reputation from the spot and by the end of his career he had been successful 36 times from 44 attempts. Sherwood saved and Cardiff won 1-0 as a result.

Another interesting point from a spot-kick awarded against Liverpool comes from a game in January 1935 when Eddie Hapgood's original effort was blocked by Arthur Riley but was then headed back past the stricken keeper by him.

William Perkins

Possibly the first great keeper Liverpool had on their books arrived from Luton Town in 1898. Harry Storer was the recognised number one but injury gave Perkins a chance he refused to let slip through his grasp. He saw out the last five games of the 1899-1900 season in this capacity. He conceded a number of goals including five in the final game of the campaign against Aston Villa. Liverpool had just completed a hectic schedule of games and were pipped to the title by Villa as a direct result. He began the following term as the man in charge of the gloves but exchanged places with Hardy a number of times until the elder man left Anfield. His time as Liverpool keeper was ultimately as limited as his predecessors and with the 1902-03 season still young he was replaced by Peter Platt. He managed a few more games before the season's end but was forced to concede defeat and move on not long after.

The Pitch

The current measurements of the Anfield pitch are 111yds x 74yds.

PFA Player of The Year Awards

There can be no greater accolade than being picked out as the best by your peers. The Professional Footballers' Association honours the best player over a season by ballot with votes cast by its members. Four Liverpool players have received this honour. Terry McDermott was the first in 1980. Kenny Dalglish followed three years later. Ian Rush was bestowed the award 12 months later on the only occasion the trophy has been retained by Liverpool players. John Barnes was the last winner in 1988. The players' union also gives the Merit Award for those who have provided outstanding service to the game. Bill Shankly was honoured in 1978. Bob Paisley was similarly rewarded on his retirement in 1983.

Points

No team has ever scored more points than The Reds in a league season. Under the two points for a win system Liverpool claimed 68 from a possible 84 in the 1978-79 campaign. Since victory has earned a three point reward Liverpool's record tally is 90. This was achieved during the sensational 1987-88 season and equalled the best ever total which was held by Everton.

Programmes

For over 50 years Liverpool and Everton shared their match day programmes. Until 1904 this took the form of a simple card listing the expected line up and the rest of the season's fixtures. The team not playing at home would chart the progress of their reserves on the flip side. A programme similar to the modern day edition was published after this date.

Usually consisting of 24 pages it also detailed the day's teams and remaining fixtures as well as general items such as theatre reviews and adverts. The front cover had a football with Everton written across it. The other edge also had a football on but this time bearing the name of Liverpool. In 1905-06 when The Reds won the league and The Blues picked up the FA Cup the cover also featured a player from each camp shaking hands. The Liverpool man held the championship trophy. The Evertonian had the FA Cup.

The First World War saw the programme reduce to a single folded piece of paper. It returned to the booklet style following the allied victory even if a little smaller in page numbers.

When the clubs decided to print their own match programmes in 1934 it created more room for in-depth features on players and games. At this time Liverpool started to put photographs on the front cover. The programme has kept pace with the rapidly increasing up turn in the club's affluence and the quality of technology available to publishers. This has seen it grow into a something resembling a a mini-magazine over the intervening years.

Promotion

The Reds boast the second longest residency in English football's top division. Their elevation following the Division Two title win in 1962 marked the club's fifth and last promotion. Despite this feat being achieved by championship success on each occasion the first couple required Liverpool to come through play off style 'test matches'. In 1894 this took the shape of a one off game with Newton Heath held at Anfield and home advantage was made to pay with a 2-0 victory. Instant relegation followed promotion and then promotion once more. This time the route to the First Division was a little more arduous. Three teams would be competing for the one spot available. As Second Division

Champions Liverpool would play the bottom clubs from the first division - Small Heath and West Bromwich Albion over two games. The first match against Small Heath finished 4-0 to the Anfield club. A no score draw followed in the away leg played 48 hours later. The players had a similar break between fixtures for the next tie as Liverpool triumphed 2-0 at home before losing the game at West Brom by the same score. Despite this set back a place in the top flight was the reward for the players' endeavours. Small Heath who had gone up with Liverpool in that first promotion made the opposite journey.

With the exception of a single season The Reds retained their place in the higher echelons of the league structure for the best part of four decades. The 1904-05 campaign saw Liverpool set the pace from day one as they rocketed towards the second division crown which was followed by the League Championship the following term. A result of the club's poorest ever season in 1953-54 was to send them tumbling down once more. It took the players a season or so to find their feet as a mid-table finish to that first term back in the Second Division shows. Automatic promotion was now the accepted way of deciding the ups and downs. The top two going up and the bottom two going down. In the six seasons which followed Liverpool finished fourth twice and third on four occasions. A run which ended in the aforementioned Second Division championship in 1962.

Bob Pursell

Scottish full-back Pursell clocked up 99 league appearances for The Reds after signing from Queens Park in 1911. Liverpool were one of many clubs interested and so keen were the Anfield board to secure their man that they decided to sign him before all the paperwork was correctly processed. Transfer irregularities landed the club in a little hot water but Pursell was deemed to be worth it. He was one of the players found guilty of match fixing just before the First World War. He returned to Anfield following the war but made two more appearances before joining Port Vale.

Quickest Goal

The sparse nature of early football records probably make it impossible to give a definitive answer but the facts available suggest that Liverpool's quickest ever goal scorer is Jack Balmer who scored after 10 seconds of the Merseyside Derby at Goodison on 16th February 1938. Other goals scored quickly after kick off in Liverpool v Everton games include Kenny Dalglish's effort after 20 seconds in September 1985. Despite racing into a 3-0 lead The Reds found themselves clinging on for dear life when the referee blew for full-time as The Blues had clawed back two goals.

Sam Raybould took a full half minute to notch the opener in January 1900. That fearsome start couldn't prevent Everton taking the spoils with a 3-1 win. Other than Merseyside Derbies the quickest Liverpool goal scorer is Paul Walsh who grabbed the opener against West Ham United after 15 seconds in August 1984.

Quotes

The club has had its fair share of quick wits. Most notably the great Bill Shankly. A few Liverpool related quotes highlight the point and the simple nature of the Liverpool way:

Bill Shankly : "Of course I didn't take my wife to see Rochdale as an anniversary present. It was her birthday. Would I have got married in the football season? Anyway, it was Rochdale reserves."

Bill Shankly: "Some people believe football is a matter of life and death, I am very disappointed with that attitude. I can assure you it is much, much more important than that."

Bill Shankly: "If a player is not interfering with play or seeking to gain an advantage then he should be."

Bob Paisley: "If you're in the penalty area and don't know what to do with the ball, put it in the net and we'll discuss the options later."

Bill Shankly: "If Everton were playing at the bottom of the garden I'd pull the curtains."

David Speedie who joined Liverpool towards the end of Kenny Dalglish's stint as manager when Liverpool were said to be in crisis: "If you think this club is in crisis you've never been to some of the places I have."

Bob Paisley: "We've had the hard times too - one year we finished second."

Bill Shankly to Tommy Smith: "You son, you could start a riot in a graveyard."

Bill Shankly when he signed Ian St John: "Son, you'll do well here as long as you remember two things. Don't overeat and don't lose your accent."

Bill Shankly to Kevin Keegan: "Just go out and drop a few hand-grenades all over the place son."

Ian Rush : "It's best being a striker. If you miss five then score the winner you're a hero. The goalkeeper can play a blinder, then let one in ... and he's a villain."

Roy Evans on Ian Rush's 600th Liverpool appearance: "He's better than Brian Lara because he's 600 not out. What a guy."

Jim Rosenthal (TV reporter): "There's nothing like second best and Liverpool certainly are not!"
Bill Shankly on Brian Clough: "He's worse than the rain in Manchester. At least the rain in Manchester stops occasionally."

Bill Shankly to Tommy Smith, who turned up for training with a bandaged knee: "Take that bandage off. And what do you mean about YOUR knee? It's Liverpool's knee!"

Bill Shankly to journalists suggesting Liverpool were in trouble: "Ay, here we are with problems at the top of the league."

Bill Shankly to a translator when surrounded by a throng of Italian journalists: "Just tell them I completely disagree with everything they say!"

Bill Shankly about the "This is Anfield" plaque: "It's there to remind our lads who they're playing for and to remind the opposition who they're playing against."

Bill Shankly to Alan Ball, who'd just signed for Everton: "Don't worry, Alan. At least you'll be able to play close to a great team!"

Bill Shankly at Dixie Dean's funeral: "I know this is a sad occasion but I think that Dixie would be amazed to know that even in death he could draw a bigger crowd than Everton can on a Saturday Afternoon."

Bill Shankly who had just been reminded that he had never played in a derby game: "Nonsense! I've kicked every ball, headed out every cross. I once scored a hat-trick; One was lucky, but the others were great goals."

Bill Shankly after beating Everton in the '71 cup semi-final: "Sickness would not have kept me away from this one. If I'd been dead I would have had them bring the casket to the ground, prop it up in the stands and cut a hole in the lid."

Bill Shankly to a Liverpool fan: "Where are you from?" Fan: "I'm a Liverpool fan from London." Shanks: "Well laddie...What's it like to be in heaven?"

Bill Shankly: "A lot of football success is in the mind. You must believe you are the best and then make sure that you are. In my time at Liverpool we always said we had the best two teams on Merseyside, Liverpool and Liverpool Reserves."

Bill Shankly: "If you are first you are first. If you are second you are nothing."

Bill Shankly: "The trouble with referees is that they know the rules but they do not know the game."

Bill Shankly to a reporter: "Yes, Roger Hunt misses a few but he gets in the right place to miss them."

Bill Shankly after signing Ron Yeats: "With him in defence, we could play Arthur Askey in goal."

Bill Shankly after a 1-1 draw: "The best side drew."

Bill Shankly after a 0-0 draw at Anfield: "What can you do playing against 11 goal posts?"

Bill Shankly after failing to sign Lou Macari: "I only wanted him for the reserves."

Jock Stein commenting on Bill Shankly: "I don't believe everything Bill tells me about his players. If they were that good they'd not only have won the European Cup but the Ryder Cup, the Boat Race and even the Grand National!"

R

Alex Raisbeck

There were few players during Liverpool's founding years that can claim to have had the influence and presence of this man. He came to Merseyside in 1898 after leaving Stoke City and was quite possibly the best centre half in the business. The fact that The Potters had successfully fought off the spectre of relegation the season before he signed for Liverpool was in no small part due to Raisbeck. He stayed at Anfield for 11 seasons and won two championship medals. Scotland also recognised his ability which secured him eight international caps. When he eventually left Anfield it was for his homeland and Partick Thistle. He returned to Liverpool following a brief managerial career and the Second World War to take up a scouting role. He died in his adoptive city in 1949 aged 71.

Sam Raybould

A prolific goalscorer who netted an amazing 31 times in 33 games during the 1902-03 season. Given his record you may wonder just how Liverpool managed to finish in fifth place that year. He scored four, including a penalty, in the 9-2 demolition of Grimsby Town and another hat-trick in the 5-0 victory over Middlesbrough. Both games were at Anfield. He finished as the club's leading scorer in four of his eight seasons. Although this would probably have been bettered had he not had an injury riddled campaign in 1903-04. He scored 127 goals from his 224 games for the club.

Jamie Redknapp

A handful of games for Bournemouth, the club his father managed at the time, had a clutch of clubs monitoring the progress of this 16 year old. Within days of his £350,000 transfer to Liverpool Kenny Dalglish placed him on the bench for a home game against Wimbledon. A 1-0 win for The Dons probably ensured he wouldn't play a part that day but just over a year later he became the youngest player Liverpool had ever fielded in Europe. It took time for the youngster to fully settle in the central midfield berth. His neat passing style and movement were obvious from the outset. The hard bitten edge many thought was absent from his game took more time to develop. Eventually very few opponents were in much doubt. Defenders also became wary of one of the best strikers of the ball. The sheer power and accuracy are the factors many goalkeepers struggle to cope with. A sad feature of his last seasons at Anfield was the sheer amount of time Jamie was sidelined by serious injury. A broken leg picked up on England duty in the summer 1997 kept him out for several months and soon after returning for his club he was plagued by niggling complaints once more. He sat out the entire 2000-01 season though did appear for the reserves during the final weeks of the campaign. He was also limited during the subsequent campaigns until his move to Spurs on a free towards the end of the 2001-02 season was agreed. He did manage to score a fine goal on his final appearance for the club at Charlton in October 2001. His final appearance in a red shirt came three days after that game. He replaced Steven Gerrard for a last five minute cameo against Borussia Dortmund in the first group stage of Champions League.

Relegation

Liverpool's first season in the First Division was not what many people had expected. Although far from title contenders it was hoped that they could at least hold their own. It ended in dismal relegation as the club finished rock bottom. Second Division champions Bury met the Reds in a one off Test Match at Blackburn's Ewood Park. The game finished 1-0 to the Manchester based outfit and saw Liverpool tumble. Elevation to the First Division was swift. A 39 year stay in the top flight was only interrupted by both world wars.

When relegation came in 1954 it was a bitter disappointment although not totally unexpected as it followed many years of mediocrity. Fortunately it was to prove the club's last.

Reserves

At any one time Liverpool's second string have been able to call upon an impressive array of talent. It is no exaggeration to say that among the up and coming hopefuls there will be seasoned professionals and internationals all turning out to keep not just match fit but hoping to stake a claim for a first team place. This may be just one of the reasons why The Reds have claimed an impressive 16 Reserve Team championships. The competition eventually sponsored by Pontins started life as the Central League. Liverpool's most concentrated spell of success came in the 1970's and 1980's during which time Roy Evans steered his squad to eight championships in ten years. A plaque awarded to the club commemorates a hat-trick of successes from 1968 -1971. The full list of championship years is as follows: 1956-57, 1968-69, 1969-70, 1970-71, 1972-73, 1973-74, 1974-75, 1975-76, 1976-77, 1978-79, 1979-80, 1980-81, 1981-

82, 1983-84, 1984-85, 1989-90.

The 1998-99 season marked Liverpool's last in the league as from that date on Premiership clubs set up their own reserve structure. Liverpool's second string became the inaugural winners of the new competition.

Tommy Robertson

A few days after making his international debut at his favoured position of outside left, Tommy Robertson joined Liverpool from Heart of Midlothian. He had won a Scottish title with the Edinburgh club and within three seasons had secured an English championship with The Reds. A goal on his debut for Scotland wasn't enough to keep him in the side and that game against Northern Ireland remained his one and only cap. However, a debut goal for Liverpool firmly cemented his place in the side until 1902 when he returned to Hearts. A skilful player with a great left foot able to crack in shots from long distance as well as set up chances for others. That second stint with his old club lasted just a few months. He moved to Dundee later in the year.

Peter Robinson

One of the most respected men in football administration Peter Robinson joined Liverpool in June 1965 as club secretary. It was a post he had filled at Brighton, Scunthorpe and Crewe Alexandra. He had also enjoyed spells in the office set up with Stockport County. In its own way his role was as demanding as the club manager's and Peter Robinson amongst many others was just as responsible for The Reds' years of domination as any of the players. Without his guiding hand the club's ability to sign the right players or have the right facilities could have been severely restricted. The Secretary is the man who organises almost every off field activity and will make some very complex day to day decisions. The job title may have changed throughout recent years - he was eventually known as the Executive Vice Chairman - but his influence was just as steady. He retired from active involvement with the day to day running of the club handing his duties to former Premier League Chief Executive Rick Parry. He remains a board member at Anfield but has since established a flourishing career as a player's agent.

Robert Robinson

Another signing from the great Sunderland side that reigned over the English game and became known as the team of talents, Robert Robinson was a forward able to score goals from any advanced position in the field. Dropping back to wing-half in 1909 blunted the amount he managed to score for the remainder of his stay at Anfield but he still managed to weigh in with regular contributions. 39 of the 65 goals he scored in a Liverpool shirt came in his first two seasons with The Reds. He was top scorer in the 1904-05 promotion season and notched 11 in the following campaign when Liverpool won the English championship.

Royal Visits

One of the first Royal visitors to Anfield were King George V and Queen Mary who attended the 1921 FA Cup semi-final between Wolves and Cardiff City. The reigning monarch Queen Elizabeth II has been to Anfield the last visit being in May 1993. Other dignitaries include Neville Chamberlain days after meeting Adolf Hitler in Munich in October 1937. Liverpool were beaten 2-1 on the day by Everton. Another Prime Minister to put in an appearance was Margaret Thatcher. Tony Blair has been to Anfield but this was before his election as Prime Minister. Fellow Labour Party leaders Michael Foot and Neil Kinnock have paid visits on match day as did President Numery of Sudan. The President is a huge Liverpool fan and the moment had great poignancy for him. Shortly afterwards he paid for the club to visit his country and take on the nation's top club side - Al Nasr.

Ronnie Rosenthal

When Ronnie Rosenthal joined Liverpool on transfer deadline day in 1990 it was on loan terms. Liverpool were stuttering towards an eighteenth championship but the Israeli's seven goals from his eight appearances turned that stutter into a confident stride. Defenders seemed to have no answers to his unpredictable style. After making a big name in his homeland he attracted the attention of many major European clubs. FC Bruges of Belgium snapped him up but sold him to fellow Belgian club Standard Liege three years later.

The move wasn't a complete success which prompted other sides to take a look at him including Luton Town and Hibernian. Both gave him trials but decided not to pursue any interest they had. Liverpool made their move and although fairly reluctant to break the club's policy of not making loan signings went with their gut instinct of the player. It didn't fail and a hat-trick away at Charlton Athletic which comprised a goal with his left foot, one strike with his right and a header was one of the many factors which earned him a permanent deal worth £1 million. He proved to be a fairly erratic player who could set the world alight one day yet turn in a relatively ordinary display a few days later. It meant that his explosive power was more often than not relegated to the substitutes bench. He furthered his reputation by obliging the manager who very often put him on as a last throw of the dice. His goal scoring knack seemed to help Liverpool live a charmed life. The fans loved him and continued to do so up until his move to Tottenham. Without doubt he still holds a place in the affection of many Liverpool fans.

The Reds waived their usual reluctance to take players on trial when it became clear this was the only way Ronnie Rosenthal's services would be secured before the transfer deadline in 1990. He scored a hat-trick on his full debut and helped Liverpool win the title with ease paving the way for a £1 million transfer.

Neil Ruddock

The man ominously nicknamed 'Razor' seemed a very un-Liverpool type player when he signed in July 1993 from Tottenham. It was his second spell at White Hart Lane Spurs had released him after little more than a season, and he went on to establish his credentials with Southampton. The chance to play for The Reds was something no player passed up lightly and for Graeme Souness the signing provided the extra steel he wanted his defence to show if they were to progress and regain their old dominance. Lapses were all too often evident in his game especially his positional and tactical acumen but when ironed out his potential was clear. Had it not been he would not have glided so effortlessly into the sweeper system preferred by new Liverpool boss Roy Evans following his appointment in January 1994. Alongside Phil Babb and John Scales The Reds had a solid defensive base on which to launch their attacks safe in the knowledge that matters at the back were safe. Long searching passes became a hallmark of Ruddock's game too.

The 1995-96 season was a little less plain sailing. Off the field issues were raised by the tabloid press and there were infamous incidents within the camp which allowed Mark Wright an opportunity to restake his claim. But throughout Ruddock was totally professional even to the extent at taking his omission from the 1996 FA Cup final team squarely on his well chiselled chin. As Neil put it he would not be: "throwing his rattle from the pram." Dominic Matteo emerged as did others to challenge the defensive hierarchy and the writing was on the wall when Ruddock was allowed a loan spell with Queens Park Rangers. Very soon after he left but not without earning his place in the affections of Liverpool fans who greatly respected his will to win - never more evenly demonstrated than in his willingness to engage in more than a little good natured antagonism with his best friend and next door neighbour Alan Shearer when the two clashed during a game.

Ian Rush

Each generation of Liverpool fans will legitimately claim that a player from their era was the finest striker the club has ever seen. Roger Hunt, Kenny Dalglish, Robbie Fowler and Michael Owen will all have a decent shout for the title but the record books say that a lean forward from the village of St. Asaph in North Wales is the best forward Liverpool has ever had. His 344 career goals for Liverpool, 58 more than the second placed Roger Hunt, include 229 in the league.

Bob Paisley saw his potential in 1980 and snapped up the youngster for £300,000. The canny Geordie showed he had psychological style akin to Bill Shankly when after a few first team games he told Rush he would never make the grade unless he was more greedy with the ball. This followed a seven game debut streak in which he failed to score. Rushie was dropped and it took him almost three months of the next season to regain a starting place. The Welshman was told that if he couldn't turn it on he would be placed on the transfer

Ian Rush - 344 career goals for Liverpool. Arguably the club's finest goalscorer.

list. It took just 17 minutes of his own season starting to open an account which saw him finish top of the club's scoring chart. The only season he didn't finish as Anfield's leading marksman before his transfer to Juventus in 1986 was the 1984-85 campaign. Although 14 goals in an injury ravaged year showed that his goal getting was largely unaffected by the set back. His best tally was 49 in the 1983-84 treble win of League, League Cup and European Champions Cup and that doesn't include a cooly taken penalty in the shoot out which decided the latter game.

Rush didn't actually leave Anfield until the season after he put pen to paper for the Turin club. They already had their quota of foreigners and so loaned him back to Liverpool for the season. Up until that time The Reds had never lost a game in which he had scored. This run was broken in the 1987 League Cup Final. Rushie provided an early lead but a double from Arsenal's Charlie Nicholas put paid to not just the record but a medal. A couple of weeks later the Liverpool number nine scored in another Liverpool defeat - courtesy of Nottingham Forest.

The player's time abroad proved to be a torrid affair and at the first opportunity Kenny Dalglish brought his old striking partner back home. The Reds kicked off the 1989-90 season with the new signing on the bench. Almost everyone expected John Aldridge to make way but he was allowed to begin as he left off the previous term. However, it wasn't too long before the Welshman was back in to the old routine himself. He fired two goals in the 1989 FA Cup Final win over Everton to match the double he scored three years earlier against the same opposition. In the process he became Liverpool's highest scorer in cup finals. By the time he finally left Anfield in 1997 he was not only the club's highest scorer in the League - his 287th and record breaking goal was the second in a 2-2 draw with Manchester United at Old Trafford - he also held the record in both domestic cup competitions. When he became available on a free transfer Kenny Dalglish reunited the manager/player partnership by taking him to Newcastle United on a short term deal. He continued to torment Everton and grabbed a vital winner in an FA Cup tie along the St James Park club's road to the final in 1998.

S

Ian St John

When this centre forward arrived from Motherwell in May 1961 he was the club's record buy. He had been set to sign for Newcastle United and even admitted he didn't know an awful lot about Liverpool but after meeting Bill Shankly decided to pick The Reds ahead of The Magpies even though the North Eastern outfit were a well established first division club and Liverpool were mid-table and a division lower. He proved an instant hit scoring a hat-trick in his first game. The opposition were Everton in a Liverpool Senior Cup tie.

Although a striker all his career he was moved to inside forward by Shanks. He took to his new role well and it didn't dull The Saint's scoring prowess

Scottish forward Ian St John cost more than double the highest sum Liverpool had ever paid when he signed from Motherwell in May 1961.

either as he not only grabbed goals himself but made them for others.

It was his extra-time goal which clinched the FA Cup in 1965. As with most of Bill Shankly's signings the new decade marked the end of his Anfield career. Before playing out his last games in South Africa Ian St John joined the exodus to Tranmere Rovers. He returned to Britain and took the managerial reigns at his old club Motherwell and then Portsmouth. A brief stint at Fratton Park preceding a coaching role with Sheffield Wednesday.

Dean Saunders

Swansea born Dean Saunders' Anfield career was so unlike that of his father. While Roy Saunders spent the best part of seven seasons on Merseyside, Dean, once the club's most costly buy at a domestic record of £2.9 million, stayed for just over a year. Everton and a number of other clubs were chasing the Derby County striker who had earned a reputation as an out and out goalscorer in a struggling team. The reason for his short-lived spell was an inability to fit into the team pattern.

Derby were battling against relegation. Teams fancied their chances against The Rams so afforded them greater space than they would normally have done. There were few better players at exploiting these gaps than Dean who could run with the ball before unleashing a ferocious shot. Liverpool couldn't and didn't play this way. Long balls over the top of advancing defences were alien to the team who preferred passing and a slower method of creation. In addition teams very rarely allowed Liverpool much space hoping to contain the play rather than charge full on to the sucker punch that could follow.

The 1991-92 UEFA Cup saw him score a club record number of goals in European competition for a season and helped bolster his strike rate to 24 from 60 games but ultimately there was little down for the player unless Graeme Souness decided to change the club's style. Dean was the type of player he would have to have build his team around as he could not slot into the smooth rhythm of his colleagues. The Liverpool manager decided to cut his losses and sold his one time star buy to Aston Villa for a £600,000 loss. Souness was confident enough to buy him once more when he was manager of Galatasaray.

Roy Saunders

For a left-half to be at Liverpool around the same time as Phil Taylor and Bob Paisley was to some extent a misfortune but it still didn't stop Roy Saunders making almost 150 appearances for The Reds. Although these days his name is probably more recognisable as the father of one time club and domestic record signing Dean Saunders who played for The Reds between 1991 and 1992. Roy

Graeme Souness whipped Derby County's prolific forward from under the noses of a number of clubs in the summer of 1991 for £2.9 million. Ultimately the move never worked for Dean Saunders who left the club just over a year later for £600,000 less.

was with Liverpool for seven seasons until he joined Swansea Town the same club where his son started his professional career and where Roy was appointed coach in 1971. The 1955-56 season was by far his most consistent with 37 league appearances and five outings in the cup. In the seasons before and after he made 28 and 27 appearances respectively with his one and only strike for the club coming during the latter campaign. The final goal of a 2-0 win at Bury in the third game of the season ensured Liverpool had both points safe as early as the 17th minute. Before joining The Reds Salford born Roy was on Hull City's books as an amateur.

Tom Saunders

Another typically unassuming member of the bootroom. Essentially his role within the team was to mount scouting expeditions - although not necessarily for players. Along with youth development duties he would run his eye over Liverpool's forthcoming opponents - particularly in European competition mounting spying missions across the continent and the UK. In addition to assessing their strengths and weaknesses Tom would establish cordial relations with the club drawn as well as checking the standards in local hotels and food in order to assess how the players would get the best rest and preparation possible.

Before taking this role he had been a headmaster who had earned his reputation within the game by managing the England Schoolboys team during the 1960s. He joined Liverpool as Youth Development officer in 1970 remaining in that post until 1986. Even after his retirement he continued to aid the club advising Kenny Dalglish during his first steps in club management. He became a director of the club in 1993 a fitting and deserved tribute to a man who had served the club quietly but efficiently for over 30 years. At the time of his death in the summer of 2001 he was still involved and had been made a vice-president of the club.

John Scales

A substitute in the 1988 Wimbledon side which beat Liverpool in the cup final he cost £3.5 million six years later after managing to establish himself in The Dons' side. He had an assurity which belied his old side's usual style and was as smooth a defender as any other in the Football League. A clean tackler who combined this feature with superb positional play in any defensive position. He was a largely defensive player with little more attacking ambition than set pieces which contributed to his 4 goals from just under 100 matches. With a more high profile club the international honours which for some reason had eluded him were finally bestowed. At any level, style or quality of football he slotted in comfortably so his release to Spurs in 1997 was something of a shock even if injury had left him struggling for total fitness and consistency. By the close of the 2000-01 season with his old team back to something like their old ways John found his life had taken an opposite twist. He was released by Ipswich Town after injury blighted his contribution to their campaign.

Scoring Feats

Although Cyril Done scored seven against Chester in 1943 and both Bill Shepherd and Don Welsh scored six in convincing victories over Wrexham and Southport respectively these were achieved in war time games. As far as the record books are concerned these do not officially count. This leaves the record number of goals scored by a Liverpool player in a single game at five. It has been achieved on five occasions by the following:

William Miller v Fleetwood R (7-0) Lancs League 3rd December 1892
Andy McGuigan v Stoke City (7-0) Division 1 January 4th 1902
John Evans v Bristol Rovers (5-3) Division 2 September 15th 1954
Ian Rush v Luton Town (6-0) Division 1 29th October 1983
Robbie Fowler v Fulham (5-0) Coca-Cola Cup 2nd Rnd, 2nd leg 5th October 1993

Thomas Bennett scored five on two separate occasions in a little over three months during the First World War games in the 1917-18 season.

Roger Hunt scored 100 goals in the fastest time. It took him a mere 144 games. When Liverpool thumped Crystal Palace in the league on September 12th 1989 it was the first, and to date only time, in league history that eight outfield players had got on to the scoresheet. Those men were (times of goals in brackets) Steve Nicol (7,90), Steve McMahon (15), Ian Rush (45), Gary Gillespie (56), Peter Beardsley (61), John Aldridge (67), John Barnes (79), Glenn Hysen (82). Aldridge's strike came with his first touch after he came on as a substitute in his farewell appearance for the club and converted a penalty.

One player has managed to score on his debut in each domestic competition and in his first game in Europe. Michael Owen had scored on his first league bow after coming on as a substitute against Wimbledon in May 1997. Three months later and exactly six minutes in to his first European game he notched the opener in a 2-2 draw with Glasgow Celtic when the British sides clashed in of that season's UEFA Cup campaign. A little over eight weeks further in to his professional career he grabbed all three in his League Cup bow as Grimsby Town were comfortably dispatched in the 4th round. He made his FA Cup debut in January 1999 when his 34th minute penalty set up The Red's 3-0 triumph over Port Vale.

Elisha Scott

A remarkable keeper with an equally remarkable Anfield career spanning almost 22 years, he could so easily have turned out on Stanley Park. His brother, Billy, was Everton's number one and after Elisha's release by Linfield he followed his elder sibling across The Irish Sea for a trial spell at Goodison. Linfield thought him too small - he stood at 5'9". Everton believed him too young for the rigours of his profession. Liverpool had no such doubts and took the 17 year old on. For a couple of seasons he played understudy to Ken Campbell but when injury forced the senior man to sit out a game against Newcastle United on New Year's Day in 1912 the teenager was thrown in at the deep end. So impressive was his display in the goal-less draw at St James Park that The Magpies attempted to sign him a few days later. Elisha, despite his obvious talent, wondered just how his future at Liverpool would pan out given the record of the man he had to oust. Campbell was a well established figure and was very well thought of not only within the game but also at Anfield, which made the keeper's role a difficult one to break into.

Newcastle's approach was rejected and the Ulsterman continued to make further inroads as he battled to earn a starting place. The early part of 1914 saw him effectively become first choice. That was a few months before the First World War broke out. The Football League was officially suspended a year later. When available the Irishman continued to turn out in war games and resumed his career once hostilities ceased. With Arthur Riley's arrival and subsequent preference it was clear that Elisha's stay at Anfield was coming to an end. This prompted Everton to try and atone for their glaring error so many years earlier. The suggested £250 deal was abandoned after furious protests by Liverpool fans. At his own request Elisha returned home as player/manager of Belfast Celtic. 22 years and 467 first team appearances for The Reds with 137 clean sheets is a record which should never be beaten and puts him head and shoulders above any keeper the club has had or is likely to have. Considering the special history the keeper's position has enjoyed that is some boast.

Scouser Tommy

The eponymous hero of The Kop's most favoured song who, during a grisly death in time of war, let everyone know exactly where his footballing allegiances lay. As his life ebbed away the lyrics tell how he extolled the virtues of not only his team but their famed bank of supporters. The words in full are as follows:

Let me tell you the story of a poor boy, Who was sent far away from his home, To fight for his King and his country, And also the old folks back home.

Well they put him in a higher division, Sent him off to a far foreign land, Where the flies swarm around in their thousands, And there's nothing to see but the sand. Well the battle it started the next morning, Under the Lybian Sun, I remember the poor Scouser Tommy, Who was shot by an old Nazi gun.

As he lay on the battlefield dying, With the blood gushing out of his head, As he lay on the battlefield dying, dying, dying, These were the last words he said:

Oh, I am a Liverpudlian, And I come from the Spion Kop, I love to sing I love to shout I get thrown out quite a lot - every week. We support a team that's dressed in red It's a team that you all know It's a team that we call LIVERPOOL And to glory we will go.

We've won the league, we've won the cup And we've been to Europe too. We played The Toffees for a laugh And left them feeling blue 5-0

The Screen Sport Super Cup

Liverpool are the only winners of this tournament designed to occupy those English teams who would have qualified for European competition but for the ban following the riot at the Heysel Stadium. The preliminary league games from which the winners of each division of three teams would qualify for the final took place during the 1985-86 season. Not surprisingly Liverpool and Everton finished top of their respective divisions. When the trophy was contested the following term, most first team regulars sat them out. Liverpool took the first leg 3-1 at home and the return tie 4-1. Ian Rush scored five over the two games.

Season's Bests

Most League points: (2 for a win) 68 Division 1, 1978-79
Most League points: (3 for a win) 90 Division 1, 1987-88
Most League goals: 106 Division 2 1895-96
Highest League scorer in a season: Roger Hunt, 41, Division 2, 1961-62
Highest scorer in a season: Ian Rush 49, 1983-84

Bill Shankly

Born in the Ayrshire mining village of Glenbuck which produced a remarkable 49 professional footballers during the late nineteenth and early twentieth century including Bill and his older brothers. After a career which saw the Scot turn out for Carlisle United and Preston North End as well as earn 7 international caps for Scotland he decided to try his hand at management. Again Carlisle United gave him his first opportunity but his route to Anfield was a complex one which took him through Grimsby, Workington and Huddersfield. While at the Yorkshire club he decided to blood a young striker by the name of Dennis Law. The rest is history. Shanks believed that a club had to have the same drive and ambition that he held. If it subsequently proved that they didn't he simply resigned rather than work with his hands tied. He had first been interviewed for the manager's post at Liverpool in 1951 but lost out to Don Welsh. When he eventually joined the club in December 1959 The Reds were treading water in the second division. The purpose Shankly held so dear was lacking but he went about changing that and in very rapid fashion. His last game in charge of Huddersfield was against Liverpool on November 28th. The Terriers won 1-0.

Promotion to the First Division came in 1962. One year later Liverpool replaced Everton as League Champions. His philosophy on the style his players should use was a simple one - pass and move. He landed the club's first F.A. Cup triumph in 1965 which was followed by magical European exploits. The manager then set his sights on consolidating a stranglehold on the domestic game and domination abroad.

When his team seemed to have reached its peak he set about replacing them. As the 70's began even legends like Roger Hunt, Ian St John, Ron Yeats and Tommy Lawrence were axed to be replaced by men that would not only take their mantles but create their own folklore. Kevin Keegan, Steve Heighway and Ray Clemence were among the new breed and didn't let their manager down. More titles were claimed as well as the club's first European trophy - the UEFA Cup in 1973. Bill's swan song was a second F.A. Cup win in 1974 as Liverpool trounced the well fancied Newcastle United. A few months later a press conference was called to unveil a new recruit - Ray Kennedy - but before the waiting journalists could be dismissed and go back to their offices to tell the public all about it came a second announcement - the resignation of the manager. The shock of his departure was only mirrored by the reaction which greeted his death in September 1981 following a heart attack. The outpouring of grief was apparent in Anfield's first game after his funeral when a huge banner read 'Shankly Lives Forever' spread across the fans.

Jackie Sheldon

Replacing Arthur Goddard on the right wing in 1913 Jackie Sheldon at last got the chance to establish himself in the first team after playing second fiddle to Billy Meredith at Manchester United. He had made a few outings while at Old Trafford so by the end of his first season with The Reds he had more than doubled the number of league and cup games he had previously managed. Sheldon was the few Liverpool players to come out of the 1914 FA Cup final with any credit after a dazzling display of wing play in which he managed to send in many centres. By the end of the following season he had scored 16 goals from the 67 appearances he had made. A tally that was helped by the assumption of penalty taking duties. He converted the first in his second game for the club and with such clinical precision there were few players with a justifiable case for taking those duties away from him.

Perhaps his status as a former United player made it certain he would come under suspicion for the skulduggery surrounding the infamous fixed game between his old and new clubs on Good Friday 1915. He missed a penalty during the first half and became a identifiable as a prime mover, as did the man he once understudied. He remained at the club for two seasons following the war before Bill Lacey came to the fore and despite the scandal which marred the latter part of his time at Anfield he was always a popular player amongst the fans.

Cyril Sidlow

Signed from Wolverhampton Wanderers in 1946, by the time his first year at Anfield was over he had won a championship medal. The game that clinched the title against Wolves was a match Sidlow excelled in. He kept out a number of attacks and helped Liverpool secure a vital 2-1 win. International caps followed those he won during specially arranged war-time games for Wales. The goalkeeper's position is one that had become something of a problem position for Liverpool who had tried a number of combinations over the previous few seasons. Sidlow brought stability to the backline and remained first choice if injury free until November 1950. That month he made his 165th and final appearance for The Reds in a defeat by Newcastle United. Conceding four goals during a 10 minute period either side of half-time in a game Liverpool eventually lost 4-2 was enough for Russell Crossley to be brought in the starting XI and while Liverpool still enjoyed little consistency in fielding the same keeper week in week out for many more seasons it was the end of the road for Cyril at least at Anfield. A crushing blow in the switch had to be that Liverpool signed Crossley on Sidlow's recommendation.

Sir John Smith

During his 17 years as Chairman Liverpool collected 22 major trophies. The smooth off field running of the club was in no small way responsible for the many successes of the 1970's and 80's. He was voted in as Chairman in 1973 after distinguished boardroom service. In that role he had the onerous responsibility of making two of the most dramatic announcements in the club's history - the resignations of Bill Shankly and Kenny Dalglish. Although he stood down from the role in the early 1990's he stayed on as a director until his death in February 1995. Apart from his involvement with Liverpool Football Club he underlined his commitment to sport in the UK by joining committees looking at the future of British tennis as well as chairing the Sports Council and serving on the Football League's Management Committee.

Tommy Smith

A near 20 year association with the club he cheered on as a boy ensures 'The Anfield Iron' is one of Liverpool's most favoured sons. He made his debut in May 1963 in a 5-1 home win over Birmingham City. He went back to the reserves and didn't manage to gain another start until November 1964 for the 1st leg of the European Cup first round tie with Anderlecht. From that point on he never looked back. His first full season earned a FA Cup winner's medal. It proved to be the first of many triumphs as he became a defensive rock in the heart of Liverpool's defence. A true hard man he became one of the game's most respected players. His motto was a simple one - none shall pass. Although an extremely tough tackler and imposing figure on those lining up against him he was also a fair player. Not dirty just arduous.

The 1977 European Cup Final win over Borussia Mönchengladbach was supposed to be his farewell to the club but swept up on the tide of euphoria his vital goal had set up he decided to prolong his career by at least another season. The summer before the 1978-79 season saw him join John Toshack's growing band of ex-Liverpudlians at Swansea.

Known as the 'Anfield Iron' Tommy Smith was one of the toughest players of his generation. A devout Liverpool fan from his boyhood he scored the second goal in the 1977 European Cup Final.

Graeme Souness

Liverpool's midfield has felt the presence of many commanding players. Graeme Souness has a fair claim to be amongst them. Strong in the tackle, on occasions too strong, and with a shot to match his temperament. Not that aggression was the only feature of his game. When called upon he could lay off the subtlest of balls as highlighted by the delicate pass which set up Kenny Dalglish for the only goal of the 1978 European Cup Final win over Bruges. It all highlighted that there was as much grace as there was anger in the Souness game.

His departure following Liverpool's dramatic penalty shoot out win over Roma in the 1984 European Cup Final coincided with The Reds' first trophy-less season for ten years.

Some didn't see it as a coincidence. They saw Souness' absence as the prime reason for The Reds, by their own high standards, having a poor season. His desire to win was almost obsessive and was never better illustrated than in his managerial career. Free spending Glasgow Rangers, backed by an ambitious chairman intent on bringing glory back to Ibrox, tempted him away from Sampdoria. With Souness as player/manager and then just manager Rangers swept all before them domestically. Tough more or less promised a job for life and a club director when the invitation to make his return to Anfield as the new boss came his way there was no hesitation in replacing Kenny Dalglish. A common view was that the Scot's appointment would continue the glut of trophies that had come Liverpool's way in recent years. However, his three year reign was as controversial as it was turbulent. Despite an FA Cup win in 1992 the club and more importantly the players seemed to step out of the winning habit. Souness was a winner and was prepared to give his all in the drive for victory. He expected no less from those around him. It wasn't forthcoming. A fact which frustrated him as much as the Liverpool fans. Players were bought and while some had great effect others seemed to have nothing to offer. These were usually offloaded at a reduced fee or simply dropped from the starting line-up never to return. The ultimate result was an unsettled camp which even saw some players express dissatisfaction with their manager.

A growing clamour for his resignation reached its peak when a photo of the manager kissing his fiancee after Liverpool's cup semi-final win over Portsmouth in 1992 appeared in The Sun newspaper on the third anniversary of The Hillsborough disaster. The photograph appeared courtesy of an exclusive deal Souness had negotiated with the title which carried scurrilous lies about the cause of the disaster and its aftermath. A subsequent apology and a donation from the agreed fee to a local children's hospital failed to appease his critics.

Despite the club's fall from glory and constant speculation regarding his position he stayed in the post until January 1994. An FA Cup defeat at home to Bristol City finally sealed his fate. He has remained in the game taking charge at Galatasaray, Southampton, Torino, Benfica and Blackburn Rovers without enjoying too long a period of rest.

South Africa

Liverpool have had a long association with players hailing from South Africa. It all began with a tour by the national amateur side in 1925. Goalkeeper Arthur Riley and striker Gordon Hodgson decided to stay in England and sign professional forms with The Reds. Riley, the first of four South African born 'keepers to play for Liverpool, had the unenvious task of trying to dislodge Elisha Scott from between the posts. It took him three and a half seasons to finally succeed but when he made the position his own he kept it for six years preceding World War Two.

Hodgson proved an instant hit and in the 11 seasons he remained on the Anfield playing staff broke almost every scoring record in the book. Another member of the touring party, Jimmy Gray, spent the 1928-29 campaign on Merseyside but the left back could only muster one appearance. The 1930's saw Riley understudied by compatriot Dirk Kemp.

Berry Nieuwenhuys and Harman Van den Berg also came to Anfield during the decade. Berry, one of the most exciting wingers of his day, went on to make himself as firm a fixture as Hodgson. Following the war he returned to the club clocking up over 250 first team appearances. Van den Berg's stay was brief by anybody's standards. He made just a handful of run outs before returning to his homeland.

Post-war Springbok Reds include Leslie Carr and Bob Priday who made intermittent appearances from 1940 to 1945. Doug Rudham was a little more successful and earned just over 60 run outs in goal from 1954 until the beginning of the 1960's. A decade earlier Hugh Gerhardi made just 6 appearances during the 1952-53 campaign.

Although neither of the following two players made international appearances for the country of their birth Bruce Grobbelaar and Craig Johnston extended The Reds' association with the Republic.

Eddie Spicer

A brave player who threw himself into the Liverpool cause with everything he had. As left-back he often proved just what playing well for the club meant to him and very rarely allowed any opposing players through. To some extent it was his courage that cost him his career. After completing his first season as an ever present in 1950-51 he broke his leg on a pre-season tour of Sweden and so was forced to sit out the entire campaign which followed. Steve Parr and Ray Lambert filled in. For the first game of the 1952-53 season Eddie Spicer returned to the team. The lay off had not softened his edges nor forced him to ease up in his style of play. Injury limited him to 28 appearances but he was fighting fit once more by August 1953. He seemed a good bet to record another ever present season after 23 consecutive games but broke his leg for a second time in December, just six days before Christmas.

A whole hearted attempt to clear his lines had forced him to collide with his own keeper Derek Underwood and Tommy Taylor. Liverpool were under the cosh at the time and eventually lost the game 5-1. This time there was no way back for Spicer who was forced to retire. Ever popular with the fans 41,266 turned up to boost his spirits in a benefit game between when Liverpool and Everton played a Lancashire XI three years after that tragic clash.

Sponsors

In this as in so many aspects of the game Liverpool were one the first teams to realise the potential to boost funds by allowing companies to place their names on the players' shirts. In this day and age just about everything that moves, and even most things that don't around a football ground, have some logo or another slapped on it. And this may seem a strange claim to make, but when it was announced that Japanese Electronic giants Hitachi were to have their names emblazoned across the front of the famous red shirt in 1979 it was a major event and caused no end of controversy as it was the first such agreement in British league football. The deal was signed on July 24th with the strip first aired in a proper game when The Reds entertained Bolton Wanderers at Anfield. When that initial agreement ended Crown Paints took over the rights until the end of the 1985-86 double winning campaign.

They in turn were replaced by Candy - an Italian based electronics manufacturer. The Reds continued to have a strong relationship with the company despite their kit endorsement ending in 1992 as Carlsberg shirt backing was complimented by Candy's match day sponsorship for many seasons.

Steve Staunton

Very few players have been resigned by Liverpool and in recent times only Ian Rush could claim that distinction. Steve Staunton joined the legendary Welsh striker when he was recruited by Roy Evans on a Bosman style transfer before the 1999-2000 season began. The player's first spell at Anfield ended in 1991 when he joined Aston Villa for £1.1 million and despite various rumours of a return since 1995 the move never materialised. Despite a promising start to his first spell at Anfield to the time of his first departure there was a sizeable groundswell of opinion building against the left-back. Some supporters were openly critical of his game and especially his distribution which some considered to have waned drastically since his first outing in 1988. At that time it seemed he could do no wrong. Capable of covering in most positions and eventually playing in goal in place of Sander Westerveld when the Dutchman was dismissed against Everton he helped himself to a hat-trick after coming on as a replacement for Ian Rush in a Littlewoods Cup tie against Wigan Athletic. He gave solid performances which left many fans purring about his prospects and those of the club for the 1990s. His willingness to overlap on the wing provided support to the attack and also set up a number of goals due to the wicked nature of his crossing.

Despite transforming that early promise into the form many knew he held during his time at Villa Park his second spell at Anfield was brought to an end in 2001 when Aston Villa managed to negotiate a return. Gerrard Houllier decided the player played no part in his long term plans. A situation he also faced the first time he left Anfield when Graeme Souness decided David Burrows was the shape of the future. This time Christian Ziege, transformed midfielder-cum-defender Jamie Carragher and others stood in his way. The old saying that you should always look forward and never go back is perhaps advice Steve should have heeded before agreeing his brief but eventful return to Merseyside.

Willie Stevenson

Willie Stevenson came from Glasgow Rangers in October 1962. As understudy to the legendary Jim Baxter he had been given little chance to show what he could do at Ibrox. At the time Bill Shankly came in for him he was actually chewing over a move to Australia where he had been on loan. He seemed to take a little time to settle in and found his first season in England a tough one but the following term was totally different. He established a devastating partnership down the left with fellow newcomer Peter Thompson. A defender who had the essential dual qualities of being a cunning yet skilful player will always prove popular at Anfield. Stevenson was no exception. He was also a good passer when he mounted forward raids.

His time at Anfield ensured he became a member of a select group of players who have won League and Cup winners medals in Scotland and England. He was the first Liverpool player to achieve this distinction and has subsequently been joined by Kenny Dalglish. The lowest point of his stay on Merseyside has to be losing the Cup Winners Cup Final to Borussia Dortmund. After the game he freely admits to throwing his loser's medal out of the toilet windows at the venue for the final - Hampden Park. Nobody has ever come forward to say they found it. In 1967 he left the club for Stoke City as Emlyn Hughes was now the clear first choice. After half a dozen seasons in The Potteries he joined his old partner in the centre of defence, Ron Yeats, at Tranmere Rovers. He spent a season at Prenton Park before rounding off his professional career with a brief stint in the North American Soccer League.

*Scottish international Willie Stevenson was on the verge of emigrating to Australia when Liverpool
expressed an interest in signing him.*

Geoff Strong

When Arsenal boss Billy Wright decided Geoff Strong would best serve his side as a wing-half rather than as an inside forward the player knew his days at Highbury were numbered. Always ready to talk business about a good player Bill Shankly registered his interest as soon as he got wind that a move could be on the cards. 69 goals from his 125 games for The Gunners proved he was a great goalscorer. Shanks wanted to deploy his new charge in a forward position but he took time to adjust to the team and its methods after signing in November 1964. When he was deemed ready for a prolonged run in the first team Liverpool had a front pairing that few players could have separated. He won an FA Cup winners medal at the close of his first season deputising for the injured Gordon Milne which remained his only appearance in the competition until midway through his third season with the club. The following campaign saw him earn a championship medal after 21 starts plus one outing as a substitute. He also weighed in with vital goals in Europe including the goal that sealed the 2-1 aggregate win over Juventus and the strike which secured passage to the European Cup Winners' Cup final at the expense of Glasgow Celtic by the same margin of victory. Despite this he missed out on a place in the final held at Hampden Park due to a knee injury picked up in the semi-final. Though he battled against the pain to rise high above every other head in the penalty area to nod the ball home.

It was a wry twist of fate that after deciding to leave Arsenal because he wasn't preferred in the position he had occupied over four seasons he became a utility player with Liverpool filling in at almost every station bar goalkeeper during his six seasons at Anfield. He finally earned a regular place in the side at left back - a position he made his own against the claims of more accomplished players who may expect to have been given their chance over the forward-cum-defender. He left Merseyside at the age of 33 spending a couple of seasons with Coventry City before hanging up his boots and making his own niche in the club's history as a gifted player able to fill any position with a professional air.

Albert Stubbins

The popular Geordie was a legend in the North East and furthered not just his reputation but the adulation he'd previously received when he joined Liverpool. The fans loved him.

His skill, pace and sheer goal scoring knack proved he was worth every penny of the £12,000 fee paid for his services. 48 league goals over the first two of his seven seasons on Merseyside was some record. With those couple of campaigns over he decided he wanted to return home to train as his wife wasn't settling in the city. Anfield officials insisted he couldn't do that and would have to remain. It led to a stand off between the player and his employer as Stubbins refused to sign a new contract. He couldn't look for a new club as Liverpool held his registration and consequently the whip hand. After a couple of months the protest was abandoned. Unfortunately a serious injury cut his already shortened season back a little further. Set backs limited his remaining time with the club and although some claim he never quite got back to the same level he displayed upon joining the club he was still a regular on the score sheet. A hero of the late 40's and early 50's Albert Subbins still has a massive following and a well subscribed fan club.

Substitutes

The substitution is a relatively new feature of the game. Before its advent in 1965 if a player was unable to continue the remaining men would just have to soldier on. Liverpool's first replacement from the subs bench was Geoff Strong who came on for Chris Lawler in a home game against West Ham United on 15th September. He also become the first substitute to score when he squared the game at 1-1 in the 76th minute. Unlike the modern game where any three of five players can be called to the field only one substitute was allowed to be named at the time. Steve Staunton is to date the only substitute to score a hat-trick after coming on. He replaced Ian Rush in the 2nd leg of a 2nd round League Cup tie with Wigan Athletic. Liverpool already held a 5-2 lead from the home leg and although staged at Anfield the game was officially an away tie for The Reds. The Irish defender was pressed into attack and opened the scoring just before the hour mark. He rounded off his treble when he made it 3-0 two minutes from the end.

Although goalkeepers could always be named as substitutes it wasn't until the early 1990's that a designated keeper was named alongside the outfield players in domestic league and cup games. Before this time a keeper regularly sat on the bench in the Charity Shield and in European competition. Mike Hooper was the first keeper to come off the bench during a first team game. He took over from Bruce Grobbelaar during the final minutes of the 1986 Charity Shield game with Everton. David James replaced the injured Bruce Grobbelaar in a Premier League match at Leeds United in February 1994 and kept his place for the rest of the season.

Swansea City

A interesting feature of Ray Kennedy's transfer to The Vetch Field was a deal agreed between Liverpool and Swansea City. The £160,000 fee was being paid via instalments but due to financial problems a payment could not be made at the specified time. In order to stave off possible liquidation for the debt The South Wales club asked for more time to pay.

Liverpool agreed but in return placed a condition on their good will. That was for any present or future Swansea players who may be available for transfer or subject to bids from other clubs be offered to Liverpool first. The Reds would then have the right of first refusal. Swansea agreed although despite a few links and rumours the agreement has never been enforced.

T

Phil Taylor

An inside forward for Bristol Rovers, Phil Taylor was brought to Anfield in 1936 as the long term successor to Matt Busby. As good a wing half as his predecessor but with far more flair, he had just worked his way in to the side on a regular basis when the Football League was suspended. With youth on his side a return to the line-up was more or less assured and he was a vital member of the 1946-47 championship winning side displaying form that earned him England caps not too long after the title was secured. In 1953-54 Liverpool were relegated. This was also Taylor's last term in the top flight and professional football. He retired at the end of the season having become a peripheral figure. In total he made 345 appearances over 14 seasons. Had it not been for the hostilities he may well have become the first Liverpool player to have turned out more than 500 times.

Taylor accepted a job with the backroom team as he was keen to extend his association with his club. When Don Welsh resigned in 1956 he was asked to become acting manager and despite competition from other candidates he was handed the post on a full-time basis. In three seasons he came close to taking the club back up to the 1st Division guiding his side to a third and then two fourth place finishes. Poor health forced him to retire with just over a quarter of the 1959-60 campaign gone. Despite high placings in the league Liverpool had been struggling finishing some distance behind the top two sides and further cracks were displayed when The Reds were knocked out of the previous season's FA Cup by non-league Worcester City. A change was becoming inevitable as the mental anguish of failing to achieve promotion was clearly beginning to take its toll.

The Team of Macs

When Liverpool kicked off their first ever season they did so with no less than 13 Scots in the 19 man squad. Among their number were Bill and Joe McQue from Celtic, Malcolm McVean who was recruited from Third Lanark, Matt and Hugh McQueen of Leith Athletic, John McCartney of Paisley St Mirren plus Andrew Hannah, Duncan McLean and John McBride of Renton. Most of these men were first team regulars which gave the team a definite Scottish tang, hence the team becoming known as The Team of Macs. John McKenna was instrumental in recruiting these players many of whom stayed with the club and played league football.

Scots and the other Celtic nations have always formed the large slice of the Liverpool playing staff. So much so that when the club went on to claim the league and cup double in 1986 only one member of the 12 on duty was English. That man was Steve McMahon, a non-playing substitute.

Television

The Reds have achieved many feats in front of the television cameras but Liverpool and TV seem to go hand in hand. Anfield hosted the first ever Match of the Day programme when the BBC brought evening highlights of the Football League game against Arsenal on 22nd August 1964. The Reds ran out 3-2 winners courtesy of a late goal from Gordon Wallace. When colour TV broadcasts were stepped up during the late 1960s Liverpool led the way once more as the club hosted another first. A match with West Ham was the first televised in colour. The home side ran out 2-0 winners. In addition The Kop was the subject of a Panorama documentary which examined its history, its effect on the Liverpool team and the opposition at Anfield.

Further documentaries charting the adventures of the club and its fans were made during the decade. These include The Kop Flies East following the players and fans on their first trip to face an East European side. Honved of Hungary were drawn to face The Reds and the programme stands as a chronicle of the club during those exciting years.

Away from factual programmes the club or its players have featured in a host of other broadcasts. Scully penned by Alan Bleasdale and shown by Granada TV was the story of a Kenny Dalglish obsessed teenager desperate to earn a trial with The Reds and hear The Kop chant his name while wearing the hallowed number 7 shirt. Kenny Dalglish made a number of guest appearances during the series. The Liverpool born writer's breakthrough work The Boys From the Blackstuff also went out during the early eighties, and in one of the programmes Sammy Lee and Graeme Souness were present at a charity night during which the infamous Yosser Hughes decided to introduce himself to the Liverpool captain.

Another well loved and at the same time loathed TV character Alf Garnett from In Sickness and in Health attended a game between Liverpool and his beloved West Ham United. The character portrayed by Warren Mitchell accompanied the son-in-law he referred to as 'the Scouse Git' played by Merseyside born actor Tony Booth. Broadcasted scenes were actually shot during the game and the players can clearly be seen in the background as the two exchange banter.

Signed from Preston North End Peter Thompson was a tricky winger with bags of skill.
He helped Liverpool become a real force during the 1960s.

Michael Thomas

For as long as the club exists there can be very little chance that any Liverpool player will earn a distinction close to the one Michael Thomas can claim. In 1989 as the seconds ticked away in the final match of the season he scored the goal which made Arsenal champions by the most slender of margins - goals scored. The Londoners came to Anfield requiring a win by two clear goals or more to snatch a championship, which seemed destined to remain on Merseyside. That goal made it 2-0 to The Gunners.

Three years later the same player scored the opening goal of the FA Cup Final and paved the way to The Reds' triumph over Sunderland. It seemed that wherever he went he hit the heights. He had joined Liverpool for around £2 million on Friday 13th December and the ominous portents associated with that day plagued Michael Thomas throughout his six year stay with the club. For two seasons injury kept him from figuring in the manager's thoughts. A glut of midfielders and the lack of fitness and form took its toll. Constant links with other clubs, mostly continental, showed that many thought he still had a lot to offer. Roy Evans agreed and resisted all approaches. He even offered a contract extension, which after some consideration, the player accepted. However, in the summer of 1998 when his contract expired he left Anfield to link up once more with the man who brought him to Merseyside, Graeme Souness, at Portuguese giants Benfica. A torrid stay at The Stadium of Light was ended in 2000 when he returned to the English game and to London with Wimbledon.

Peter Thompson

A gifted and crafty winger who had everything - pace, skill, ball control and the ability to deliver a great cross. Bill Shankly swooped on his former club, Preston North End, for a player he knew could give his team that little bit extra. Although a mere 21 years of age the £35,000 invested in him was no gamble. He tore defences apart and set up countless goals for teammates. He was no slouch when presented with a chance himself and struck over 50 times in a Liverpool shirt. Full England caps to add to his youth honours were seen as a matter of course and so it proved. Only Alf Ramsey's decision that the use of wingers was an unnecessary luxury curtailed his international career. He left the club in 1972 for Bolton Wanderers staying at Burden Park until his retirement in 1978.

Phil Thompson

The Kirkby born defender enjoyed a dream career. He lead the club he worshipped to glory both home and abroad as well as captaining his country. Bill

*Bill Shankly once said that Phil Thompson tossed a coin with a sparrow for his legs and lost.
While his boss may have been flippant about his physique
he saw great potential in his charge and predicted a glorious career.*

Shankly confidently predicted he would do all these things while he was a fledgling professional. His debut at Old Trafford was the venue for a convincing 3-0 thrashing of Manchester United in February 1971. Regardless of all the medals he won as a player there can be little doubt that his proudest moment was being installed as the captain of Liverpool in 1979. In that role he lofted a whole host of major trophies above his head.

The defensive partnership cultivated between Alan Hansen and Mark Lawrenson eventually drew a veil over his first team chances and he was transferred to Sheffield United in March 1985. Kenny Dalglish brought him back to Anfield a year later to coach the reserves. In six seasons he guided the second string to a Central League title before Graeme Souness replaced him with Sammy Lee. A successful businessman he took various media roles before his appointment as Gerard Houllier's assistant in November 1998. In October 2001 he took over as caretaker manager following Houllier's heart surgery.

John Toshack

Cardiff City's £110,000 pay day when John Toshack signed for Liverpool in November 1970 was a club record. At 6'2" and with an impressive frame which made him deadly in the air he was the perfect foil for Kevin Keegan his striking partner for most of his Anfield career. He turned out 40 times for Wales and earned a reputation as a poet for the odes he wrote about fellow players and games. He even had some of his work published. Although he only left Merseyside during the 1977-78 campaign he could have been transferred three years earlier but after agreeing terms with Leicester City failed a medical. When Tosh left it was for the sprawling vales of South Wales and sands of Swansea. As team boss he guided The Swans from the Fourth to the First Division in five seasons recruiting many of his former teammates along the way. His long awaited return to Anfield came in October 1981. From the opposition dug out he saw his charges do him proud with a 2-2 draw. They finished sixth in that first top flight season and earned a UEFA Cup spot.

Despite their relegation a year later Tosh's managerial skills were being monitored by some of Europe's top clubs. He joined Real Sociedad and went on to Real Madrid before returning to Sociedad. A brief and highly criticised job share as the manager of the Welsh national side lasted for a single game. Kenny Dalglish's decision to resign as Liverpool boss saw him linked with a take over of the reigns at Anfield. Claims that a similar offer was put to him just prior to Gerard Houllier's arrival have also been made but he stayed in Spain to take control at Deportivo La Corunia. From there it was on to Turkey and Besitkas. The politics of Turkish football ensured his tenure was a short one. He agreed to take control at Madrid for a second time but once more found himself discarded for

*Welsh striker John Toshack formed one of the most devastating strike partnerships
the modern game has ever seen when he linked up with Kevin Keegan at the beginning of the 1972-73 season.*

failing to win the Spanish title or Champions League. St Etienne was the next continental side to send out an SOS to the Welshman. The French side were struggling to avoid relegation from the 1st Division but his short term contract was ended when Real Sociedad invited him to return once more when they too found themselves facing relegation after a poor run of results. He has since managed other continental clubs.

Tranmere Rovers

A league meeting between Liverpool and the team often referred to as "Merseyside's other club" has yet to take place. Even the cup competitions have only managed to pair the two sides together on a couple of occasions. The first being a 4th round FA Cup tie in February 1934. Although Tranmere were drawn at home they agreed to switch the game to Anfield. The Third Division North outfit were dismissed with some ease courtesy of a 3-1 victory. The next game came in the 2nd round of the 1979-80 League Cup. A creditable scoreless draw at Prenton Park left the Wirral club with some chance for the away leg. At Anfield the tie remained deadlocked until half time although any Tranmere raised expectations were dashed shortly after the interval as Liverpool opened their account. Another three goals followed over the next half hour.

The only action between the two for just over 20 years took the shape of pre-season friendlies but in the quarter-final of the 2000-01 FA Cup Tranmere and Liverpool were drawn together again. Rovers had already disposed of Everton in the 4th round with a 3-0 win at Goodison Park. Hopes of a Mersey double were high but when The Reds took control midway through the first half establishing a 2-0 lead it appeared the result was beyond question.

However, Tranmere had trailed Premiership Southampton 3-0 at the break in the previous round only to stage one of the most rousing comebacks in FA Cup history and edge through 4-3 with a hat-trick from Paul Rideout and a late winner from boyhood Red Stuart Barlow. Another Liverpool supporter Steve Yates who grabbed a brace against Everton threatened a similar recovery when he headed home just seconds into the final period. Steven Gerrard restored the two goal cushion within minutes but a goal from Wayne Allison kept it tight until Robbie Fowler secured progress to the semi-finals with a late penalty.

	P	W	D	L
Football/Premier League	2	2	0	0
FA Cup	2	2	0	0
League Cup	2	1	1	0
Others	0	0	0	0
(Charity Shield, War time games and Screen Sport Super Cup)				
Total	**6**	**5**	**1**	**0**

Transfers

Current transfer trends mean a great deal of money will usually be required to tempt some players away from their clubs. Fees started to inflate dramatically during Kenny Dalglish's reign. The legendary Scotsman proved he was no miser with the purse strings during his management days. In 1988 he not only broke the British transfer record with the £1.9million signing of Peter Beardsley in the months and days before and after that deal he bought John Aldridge for £750,000, John Barnes for a cool £900,000 and Ray Houghton for £825,000. The 1990s saw some really big money splashed around. In July 1991 Liverpool shattered the domestic transfer mark again with a £2.9million bid for Dean Saunders.

Two years later Phil Babb became the most expensive player in Anfield history following his £3.6million capture from Coventry City. Even that massive fee was almost trebled less than 12 months later when Stan Collymore ended his controversial stay with Nottingham Forest. Many clubs made offers around the £8.5million Liverpool ended up paying but Stan decided his future lay at Anfield. Dietmar Hamman's recruitment from Newcastle United before the start of the 1999-2000 season forced Liverpool to part with a similar amount but the club record of £11 million for Emile Heskey was completed during the spring of 1999. Despite this huge sum the figure is some way off the current record between domestic clubs created by Rio Ferdinand's departure for Old Trafford. The £30 million paid by The Magpies makes even that fee look like small beer but ensures that if Liverpool were to threaten that price tag the man responsible would have to be a special player.

A strange feature of The Reds' transfer history is that very few players who have arrived for big money have commanded a higher fee on their departures whilst still in their prime.

The Treble

But for a freak goal which cannoned off Jimmy Greenhoff's chest during the 1977 FA Cup final Liverpool fans could have been celebrating a treble of the game's three ultimate prizes.

The League Championship secured before Wembley was followed up by The European Cup four days after that disappointment. It took another seven years for The Reds to secure three trophies in the same season for the first time when the League title, European Cup and League/Milk Cups were won in Joe Fagan's first season as manager. Gerrard Houllier had been employed a little longer when Liverpool became the first English side to win three cups in the same campaign. Without a trophy for six years Liverpool treated themselves to both domestic prizes on offer plus the UEFA Cup. All were won after thrilling finishes.

The Worthington Cup was settled via a tense penalty shoot-out with Birmingham City, the FA Cup with a Michael Owen double completed just two minutes from time edged The Reds past Arsenal who took the lead with a quarter of an hour to go. The UEFA Cup was finally won 5-4 with an own goal from Alaves defender Geli four minutes from another penalty competition. The Reds had stormed to a 2-0 lead only to see a goal pulled back. Their two goal cushion was regained just before half-time but the scores were brought level at 3-3 soon after the break. Liverpool made it 4-3 before the Spanish side equalised moments from the final whistle.

Geoff Twentyman

Geoff Twentyman had already played close to 200 games for Carlisle United before joining Liverpool in December 1953. His promise was clear for all to see. Twentyman was a powerful player who never quite knew when he was beaten. At Brunton Park he had operated as a centre-half but found life at Anfield understudying Laurie Hughes difficult. So accomplished was Hughes that the younger man had very little chance of dislodging him. In his early times with the club he played at left-half. An ever present in the 1955-56 season he scored seven goals and two years later took over as captain for a short spell. Twentyman was one of the few players to come away from the humiliating FA Cup defeat by Worcester City in the 1958-59 season with any credit after scoring Liverpool's goal from the penalty spot. Yet, he was deemed to lack the genuine class necessary if Liverpool were to be promoted and was replaced by Tommy Leishman.

During the 1959-60 season he was allowed to join Ballymena United as player manager. Three years later he returned to Carlisle United to play a handful of games before dropping outside the league structure to play for Penrith and Morecambe. He returned to Anfield in 1967 as chief scout, a job he held for almost 20 years before he was replaced by Ron Yeats.

U

UEFA Cup

Liverpool won the trophy at their first two attempts. In 1972-73 The Reds took on Borussia Monchengladbach in the two leg final. Spurs had been squeezed out of the last four on the away goals rule and the margin of victory in the final was just as tight. An impressive 3-0 home victory in the first game proved vital as the Germans took the 2nd leg 2-0 clinching Liverpool a nail biting aggregate win.

Three years later Belgian outfit Club Brugge KV pushed The Reds just as hard. Liverpool were in confident mood following a well deserved victory over Barcelona including a 1-0 win at The Nou Camp. It was an historic win as The Reds became the first club to topple the Spanish giants on their home ground in all European competitions. Brugges shocked a packed Anfield by racing into a 2-0 lead. However, backed by their vociferous home support Liverpool turned the game around in a magical five minute spell which saw Ray Kennedy, Jimmy Case and Kevin Keegan make it 3-2. Keegan provided an early lead in the return game and although the Belgians equalised soon after they could not stop Liverpool claiming the trophy again courtesy of a 4-3 aggregate win.

A match ticket provides a souvenir of the treble clinching game.

The majority of the club's most recent travels in the UEFA Cup haven't been as fruitful. The 1991-92 campaign (Liverpool's next after that 1976 triumph) seemed encouraging during the early rounds and even stirred up memories of past European glories following the 3-2 aggregate victory over Auxerre. The French side led 2-0 from the 1st leg of the 2nd round tie which meant that Liverpool had to score at least three goals to book passage to the next stage. An expectant yet nervous Anfield crowd witnessed one of the best games for decades as The Reds went about their task. A Mark Walters' goal six minutes from time made the score on the night 3-0. Unfortunately neither the fans nor the players could repeat the feat against Genoa at the quarter final stage. The Italians also held a 2-0 lead before an Anfield return but despite a exhibition of similar fervour to that against Auxerre a 2-1 win for the visitors marked the end of the trail.

The 2000-01 campaign, the club's first European outing since 1999, was a different matter. Liverpool looked far from convincing during the early stages of the competition but still progressed at the expense of Rapid Bucharest and Slovan Liberec of The Czech Republic. From the 3rd round onwards teams parachuted in after losing out in the early stages of the Champions League became possible opposition. Greek outfit Olympiakos were such a side. Liverpool took a 2-2 draw back to Anfield but eased through to a showdown with former European Cup foes Roma. Their home stadium had hosted two glorious European Cup final wins and always proved a luck venue but with Roma, said to be the form side in Europe Roma topped the Italy's Serie A by a huge margin and pundits predicted a humiliating end to Liverpool's adventures.

However, a 2-0 win in the Olympic Stadium, courtesy of clinical Michael Owen strikes, set up a quarter-final tie with Porto.

The Portuguese side were unable to cope with Liverpool who were rampant in the 2nd leg at Anfield. The last four set up a mouth watering tie with Barcelona. The Catalan giants were stifled in The Nou Camp as Gerard Houllier's side stuck to a conscious plan to blunt the Spaniards in attack. Critics lined up to blast The Reds' negative tactics but a Gary McAllister penalty just before half time in the return leg saw Liverpool through to the final in Dortmund against surprise finalists Deportivo Alaves. Although little was known about the side enjoying their first European odyssey Liverpool's preparation seemed to be paying off as The Reds raced to a 2-0 lead after goals from Markus Babbel and Steven Gerrard within 15 minutes. Alaves pulled one back with a header only for Gary McAllister to restore Liverpool's two goal cushion with a penalty just before the break.

Deportivo squared the game within five minutes of the restart with a header and free-kick. Robbie Fowler left the bench and seemed to have settled the game quickly after his introduction. However, former Manchester United player Jordi Cruyff levelled once more two minutes before the end to take proceedings into extra-time. A golden goal during the 30 minutes would decide the tie. Both sides had the ball across the line only for the referee to rule the efforts out for offside. A late sending off made The Spaniards more cautious in their approach but The Reds continued to plug away. A foul on Vladimir Smicer just outside the area led to another red card. Gary McAllister lined the resulting free-kick up looking to put the ball deep in to the area towards the players Liverpool had sent up but a deflection from Alaves defender Delfi Geli hit the back of the net to make the final score 5-4.

Unbeaten Runs

In the year of the club's acceptance to the Football League Liverpool claimed the Second Division crown remaining unbeaten for the entire 28 game campaign. That record remained unparalleled for almost 100 years. The 1987-88 term saw the club equal Leeds United's record of remaining without a league defeat from the start of a season. The Yorkshire club went on a 29 game run 15 years previously. Alan Clarke an integral member of Leeds' squad saw his younger brother Wayne halt The Reds attempt to claim the mark as their own. Clarke Jnr scored the only goal in the 30th match - away at Everton.

The club's best run without losing at home is 85 games - 65 in the league, 9 in the League Cup, 7 European games and 6 in the FA Cup - between 21st January 1978 and 31st January 1981.

Upsets

Perhaps the most humbling moment in Liverpool's FA Cup history came in 1959. Billy Liddell was dropped for the visit to tiny Worcester City. However, Liddell's absence could hardly be cited as the reason for The Reds crashing out. The non-league side made the most of their chances and ran out 2-1 winners. Geoff Twentyman scored seven minutes from time but it was far too late to help The Reds salvage anything from the game.

Defeat more or less hastened the departure of manager Phil Taylor. Although he was left in the post for the next ten months it was very clear that his time at the helm needed to be concluded if the club was to progress. Bill Shankly, the man who replaced him has written himself into Anfield folklore but even he succumbed to the might of a giant killer. Despite being stretched in the earlier rounds and having to make the long trek to Vicarage Road Liverpool entered into a quarter-final tie with Watford as strong favourites to progress to the last four. The Hornets were battling against relegation to the third division but managed to pull off a 2-0 victory which rocked the footballing world but Shanks himself.

V

Barry Venison

The story of how Barry Venison joined Liverpool should have earned him a contract for sheer initiative and to some extent his pure cheek. Although he had captained Sunderland in the 1986 League/Milk Cup final and in the process became the youngest ever player to captain a Wembley side he was seen as an ordinary journeyman with little chance of playing for one of the biggest clubs in Europe let alone England. But that was far from Barry's contention a fact he made known when a letter from the player landed on top of Kenny Dalglish's in-tray. The missive asked whether Liverpool would like to enjoy the benefit of his services. The £250,000 deal that it sparked was a decent gamble for Liverpool who at the very least required defensive cover following the departure of Phil Neal. Jim Beglin and Steve Nicol were operating as full-backs but with Nicol able to cover any position on the field it gave the manager some depth in reserve.

The North Easterner started the 1986-87 season as the first choice right back with both Beglin and Nicol ruled out. But even when both returned to fitness he was still retained in some capacity making 33 league appearances including two from the bench. He made a return to Wembley in the League/Littlewoods Cup final but again left on the losing side. His participation in The Reds' 1987-88 campaign was curtailed due to an achilles injury and with Steve Staunton, David Burrows and Gary Ablett forcing their way in to the side it seemed the task of returning would be an arduous one. Although his number of appearances were limited over the next two seasons for various reasons he still won FA Cup and League Championship medals. Firmly established in the Liverpool side he found himself edged out of the picture when Graeme Souness took over as manager and was sold to Newcastle United for the same amount as he had cost The Reds six years earlier. At St James Park he went from strength to strength even earning England caps in 1994 at the age of 30. There was a brief link-up with the man who allowed him to leave Anfield at Galatasaray. He finished his career at Southampton and emerged as a TV presenter after cutting his media teeth as a pundit with Sky Television.

Victories

Record League win: 10 - 1 v Rotherham T Division 2 18th February 1896.

Record cup win: 11 - 0 v Stromsgodset Drammen European Cup Winners' Cup 1st Rnd 1st leg 17th September 1974.

The Reds' best margins of victory in other major competitions are listed below:

FA Cup: 8 - 0 v Swansea City 2nd Rnd Replay 9th January 1990.

League Cup: 10 - 0 v Fulham 2nd Rnd 1st leg 23rd September 1986.

European Cup: 10 - 1 v Oulu Palloseura 1st Rnd 2nd leg September 1980.

Inter City/UEFA Cup: 10 - 0 v Dundalk Fairs Cup 1st Rnd 1st leg September 1969.

W

Walter Wadsworth

Spotted playing as a local amateur Liverpool wasted no time in recruiting Wadsworth as a centre-half. He made just one appearance before the First World War in a 3-0 defeat at Middlesbrough. Despite that setback he matured into a defensive rock during the 1919-20 season and was an ever present member of the side during the following campaign. He also enjoyed a good season at the other end of the pitch scoring five goals. It just got better and better as he helped The Reds secure back to back titles from 1921-23. David Pratt eventually managed to work his way into the side by the turn of 1925 and during the same season had limited his adversary to just four games. A move to Bristol City allowed him to keep playing as did a spell at New Brighton. He finally retired in 1936. Midway though his Anfield career Wally's brother Harold became a member of the same side although the two played together very rarely. Winger Harold made just 54 appearances over five years. Walter Wadsworth made 240 outings for Liverpool.

John Walker

One of Scotland's most accomplished internationals by the time he joined Liverpool in 1897 John Walker was a tricky inside-forward able to create as many goals as he managed to convert. 31 in just over 133 appearances was a respectable return over the five seasons he spent on Merseyside before returning to Scotland and helping Rangers lift the Scottish FA Cup.

He had more or less secured the title for Liverpool back in 1901 by scoring the winner in the final game of the season against West Bromwich Albion. Sunderland led the table before the game on goal average so a draw or a win was essential for Liverpool. Walker eased nerves with an early strike which his side were able to defend.

Mark Walters

Always keen to recruit players he knew and trusted Graeme Souness bought Mark Walters from former club Glasgow Rangers just prior to the 1991-92 season beginning. Whether the signing was a pre-emptive decision to replace John

Barnes remains a mystery. More likely that Walters was bought due to the number of match winning performances he had turned in at Ibrox. It was form he never recaptured on Merseyside. There were high points, occasions when his range of tricks bamboozled opponents and won games. His goals too could be memorable including the winner against Auxerre in the 1990-91 UEFA Cup tie which Liverpool won despite trailing 2-0 after the 1st leg. Walters slid home the effort which made it 3-0 at Anfield six minutes from the end guiding The Reds through. Days like this were few and far between and when he was used it was usually as a late substitute when The Reds needed something different in order to change the course of a game. Soon after becoming manager Roy Evans decided Walters was a luxury his side could no longer afford. After extended loans with Stoke City and Wolves he was allowed to join Southampton on a free in 1996.

The War Years

When the First World War started in 1914 it took the best part of two years for the powers that be to suspend play within the Football League. Teams kept playing but in essentially pointless contests. From September 1915 to April 1919 two competitions were played out - The Lancashire Section Principal Tournament and The Lancashire Section Supplementary Tournament. Liverpool claimed the Principal Championship in 1917 and the subsidiary/supplementary title in successive seasons: 1917-18 and 1918-19.

The advent of World War Two was a totally different matter. The possible repercussions of an all out conflict with Hitler's Germany were plain for all to see. It meant that the 1939-40 league campaign was just three games old when abandoned. Regional divisions were set up once more but unlike those established during the previous hostilities allowed many changes to both the rules of the game and personnel to ensure Ministry of Defence guidelines on travel, crowding and air raids were satisfied. Guesting, a system which allowed professionals to turn out for teams close to their military postings was introduced. It allowed a number of star names to turn out for Liverpool including Cliff Britton, Sam Bartram, Stan Cullis and Tom Finney. A teammate of Finney's at Preston North End, a Mr W Shankly, made his one and only appearance in a red shirt during the 1941-42 season.

In as much as these things matter Liverpool finished top of the second period of The Football League North which ran from December 1942 to May 1943. Tom Cooper, the club's full back and England international, was the only Liverpool player to die during active service when his army motorcycle collided with a bus.

Tom Watson

Although the Victorian era is assumed to be something of a dour age Tom Watson is one man who could be said to have bucked the trend. In some ways his personality could be likened to that of Bill Shankly's. In December 1909 Newcastle visited Anfield and totally dominated the opening exchanges. They cruised into the 5-2 lead they had at the break as soon as the whistle went Watson implored his opposite number to make sure his players kept the score down. Unable to watch the remaining action Tom Watson decided to stay in his office and was only coaxed out when his charges levelled at 5-5. This allowed him to see Arthur Goddard's winner give The Reds a very unlikely victory. He spent 19 years at Anfield and proved a tough act to follow for many of his successors. Only his death in 1915 split him from the club he had guided to a first league championship and FA Cup Final appearance.

Weather

By far the most notorious game to be abandoned due to the conditions was the visit of Borussia Mönchengladbach to Anfield in the 1st leg of the 1972-73 UEFA Cup final. The game was called off after half an hour due to torrential rain. During the play that had been possible Bill Shankly detected that the German side looked vulnerable in the air. Brian Hall had initially been selected but when the game finally took place 24 hours later he was relegated to the substitute's bench, taking the seat vacated by John Toshack. Tosh's aerial threat was never underestimated by the canny Scot and it proved a sound decision. Even though the towering Welshman failed to find the net himself his very presence had the desired effect. Liverpool romped to a 3-0 win, eventually lifting the trophy 3-2 on aggregate.

For the 2nd leg of the European Cup quarter final with Cologne in March 1965 the usually lush Anfield turf was covered in thick piles of snow. Once the players emerged for the knock around it was clear to the referee that the game could not take place. Just over a year later a confident Liverpool set about taming Dutch champions Ajax in the 2nd round of the same competition. The Amsterdam weather was atrocious. Fog restricted visibility to little more than 50 yards. FIFA rules that the referee should be able to see both goals were disregarded after the home officials persuaded the man in black he only needed to see each end of the pitch from the centre circle. The match was farcical. Liverpool lost 5-1 and at one stage Bill Shankly roamed around the pitch to gee up his players. Nobody apart from those around the men he spoke to even saw him.

Luton Town gained a notorious reputation with many Liverpool fans in the late 80's and not just for their hideous plastic pitch. It was January 1987. As cup holders and double winners The Reds were expected to do well in this year's FA Cup competition. The Hatters provided the first hurdle and although they were also in Division One progress at their expense seemed a good prospect.

When the first game ended 0-0 an Anfield replay was scheduled to take place a few days later. Crowds had already gathered for the game when news spread about its postponement. Although cold the Merseyside skies were virtually clear. The same could not be said for the south of England. The Luton party were snowed in at Stanstead Airport. As a consequence their early evening flight was cancelled. It was a bitter disappointment. Liverpool gave a thoroughly professional display at Kenilworth Road and when the second game eventually took place The Reds threw everything at the visitors who managed to hold on thanks to the woodwork, a handful of good saves, dubious use of the offside flag and sheer luck. The referee tossed a coin to decide which club would host the second replay Luton called correctly. A heartbreaking 3-0 victory put The Hatters through to the next stage.

Wembley

The national stadium earned the nickname of Anfield South among the Liverpool faithful due to the amount of visits the club has paid to it. Including both major domestic cups, Charity Shields and the 1978 European Cup Final The Reds had appeared at Wembley 30 times before its demolition.

Alf West

Like many Yorkshiremen Alf West was a tough guy who hated giving what he had earned away lightly. These were qualities a full-back needed in abundance. Liverpool have boasted a list of hard yet far from dirty defenders and West was one of the first on that distinguished list. He joined the club from Barnsley in 1903 and pitched in to a below par side that had been demoralised by five consecutive defeats. Liverpool narrowly won that debut game but a lot of damage had already been done and relegation was more or less a certainty from early on. Next season he was out of the team until December but played in 16 of the final 19 league games helping the club achieve promotion at the first attempt.

When Liverpool toasted their championship victory 12 months later Alf West had made 37 appearances and scored three penalties. Any chance of repeating the feat was wrecked four games in to the next campaign when a bad eye injury kept him out for the rest of that season.

Once more the player returned and made 33 appearances but when the 1908-09 season kicked off he was out of the starting XI once more and managed just 10 games spread sporadically throughout the term. Reading made overtures and successfully recruited West but within 12 months he had rejoined Liverpool. With Eph Longworth occupying his old role chances were going to be few or far between. He was restricted to four outings as cover for Crawford at left back before another transfer this time to Notts County.

Matters were a little better at County than they had been at Reading and a 2nd Division Championship medal in 1914 was a high point.

Johnny Wheeler

Bootle born Johnny Wheeler took the scenic route to Anfield via Tranmere Rovers and Bolton Wanderers. But clubs were served with distinction in well over 100 appearances for each. He had earned an England cap and was a member of the Bolton team which lost the 1954 FA Cup final after leading Blackpool 3-1. The game was renamed the 'Matthews Final' in recognition of the winger's contribution to a comeback which settled the game at 4-3 to The Seasiders. Two years after that game he became one of Phil Taylor's first recruits. With such a pedigree it was easy to see why. He was a good player and at 28 years of age possessed a wealth of experience and he still had much to offer a team. Especially one struggling to break free of the 2nd Division. Five games into his Anfield career he scored a hat-trick in five minutes. Liverpool were level at 1-1 with Port Vale with just nine minutes left at Anfield. The game looked to be heading for a draw until Wheeler stepped in to earn Liverpool both points.

He scored just 20 goals for the club over the five seasons he could justifiably be called a regular and if there was one drawback to his play it would have to be his speed off the mark which at inside-right could leave his defenders struggling if the opposition gained possession and had found very little resistance from Wheeler. During the 1958-59 season he was Liverpool captain but handed the job over to Ronnie Moran the following season. Moran was actually Wheeler's cousin. Injury limited his chances throughout his last three seasons at Anfield and throughout the 1961-62 promotion campaign he managed just one outing - a home game with Plymouth Argyle in December. Gordon Milne had assumed his mantle and realising that the younger man had a few qualities he did not Wheeler decided to call it a day still aged 33. A little after retiring he became coach and then assistant manager at Bury.

Ronnie Whelan

Not long after his 18th birthday the Irishman found himself leaving Home Farm for the heady heights of English and European giants Liverpool. A modest fee changed hands for a player who made a huge impact and earned a reputation for scoring important goals. His debut effort against Stoke City was followed by two in the 1982 Milk Cup win over Spurs. He followed that up with a curling shot in the 2-1 victory over Manchester United in the 1983 final.

Only injury robbed him from being a permanent fixture in the Liverpool midfield for well over a decade. Following Alan Hansen's retirement he was the natural successor as club captain. His stint as a stand in during Hansen's absence equipped him with the experience and showed him to be a natural leader.

When he left Liverpool in 1994 it was to become player/manager of Southend United. Relegation to the Third Division in 1996 ended that appointment. He became manager of Greek outfit Panionious whom he steered to the quarter finals of the European Cup Winners Cup in 1999.

Dick White

The first great Liverpool player of modern times to sign from Scunthorpe United, with Ray Clemence and Kevin Keegan to follow. Laurie Hughes was so firmly ensconced in the side that Dick White took a few years to stake his claim for a place in the line-up that always threatened to return to the 1st Division but never quite managed it. White like so many players that had got The Reds so close to the promised land left Anfield following the 1961-62 promotion clinching campaign. Having just completed his eighth season with the club and making just over 200 appearances he recognised there were younger men ready to take his place. But for the intervention of Bill Shankly he could have left a season earlier. His preferred position of centre-back had been assumed by Ron Yeats as had the club captaincy Dick White had held for just over a year. A move to right back saw him replace John Molineux who lost his place but by the summer of 1962 it was clear that Gerry Byrne would be the long term solution to the manager's defensive plans.

A no nonsense player who mainly concentrated on his duties of repelling forwards he scored just one goal. A vital strike in the 3-2 FA Cup win over Southend. Liverpool got off to a good start scoring as early as the opening minute but the expected rout of the lower league outfit never materialised and the narrow defeat was more than the minnows deserved.

White scored the second. He left Anfield for Doncaster Rovers playing approximately three seasons for the South Yorkshire club before accepting the manager's job at non-league Kettering Town.

World Club Championship

This invitational event is usually contested by the champions of the European and South American continents. It has proved poor hunting ground for The Reds. In their two appearances Liverpool haven't so much as scored a goal. In

1981 crack Brazilian outfit Flamenco provided the opposition. A disappointing 3-0 defeat was followed up by further misery three years later when Independiente of Argentina notched an early lead which they managed to hold on to. Both matches were played in Tokyo, Japan.

Dave Wright

Had it not been for the presence of Gordon Hodgson Dave Wright could well have been recognised as one of The Reds most prominent strikers of the 1930s. Ideally built for the job, the stocky yet skilful forward scored 35 from exactly 100 games and in his two seasons as a regular finished second best to Hodgson with 13 strikes during the 1931-32 season and 14 the following campaign. After spending many years with Sunderland he made his debut for The Reds at inside left and remained there until asked to play a more thorough supporting role. The signature of Sam English saw the balding Wright moved back to his unfavoured slightly deeper position. He lasted just one more season and 12 games before seeking a move. Hull City answered his call but he spent a brief time there as he eventually did at Bradford where he finished his playing days in 1936.

Mark Wright

Derby County's relegation at the close of the 1990-91 season ensured their two stars, Mark Wright and Dean Saunders, would have to seek a future elsewhere. The Rams were able to capitalise on two multi-million pound assets, and were touting their skipper and established England international before the drop. Liverpool were first in the queue once the sale doors opened. Wright began his career at Oxford United during the 1981-82 season but left the Manor Ground to join Southampton after just 10 games.

Despite the relatively humble surroundings in which he played, and that centre backs such as Terry Butcher had dominated the England set up for many years he was in Bobby Robson's thoughts receiving his first cap in 1984 and going on to play and score in the 1990 World Cup finals held in Italy. Cruelly he missed the chance to play in Mexico four years earlier after breaking his leg in the FA Cup semi-final against Liverpool.

The £2.2 million buy was immediately installed as captain taking over from Ronnie Whelan. His aerial presence was an initial benefit to The Reds who had struggled to deal with the high ball into the area over the past few years from either open play or set pieces. Liverpool also seemed to have a successor to the centre-back dynasty that had began with Ron Yeats and seemingly stalled once Alan Hansen and Mark Lawrenson retired.

By the end of his first season Wright had achieved the dream of leading his side up the 39 steps to the Royal Box at Wembley and holding the FA Cup aloft. The emotion and honour of the occasion was clear for all to see.

A series of niggling injuries limited his chances over the next couple of years and the feelings of Roy Evans who took charge of team affairs in 1994 were further handicaps. During the summer it seemed his Liverpool career was in tatters. The manager questioned both his fitness and attitude when he left him out of the club's pre-season tour to train with the reserves and youngsters. With Neil Ruddock already at the club plus John Scales and Phil Babb being brought into the fold to play in a three men at the back sweeper system which they operated to perfection, the future looked bleak.

If motivation really was a problem Wright demonstrated he could tap into a huge pool of it and when injury presented him with another chance he took it and was acclaimed as The Reds' best defender over the 1996-97 and 1997-98 campaigns. The possibility of further England caps was mooted and eventually happened, but injury proved to be his Waterloo not long after and forced him into a premature retirement. Still located on Merseyside he took control of struggling Conference outfit Southport and is currently in charge of Chester City.

Tom Wyllie

Liverpool's first signing following the split with Everton. Where he officially arrived from is unknown. Speculation is that he may have been signed directly from Everton but he could possibly have arrived via Glasgow Rangers the team he played prior to moving to England. He was the outside or inside right of the team which won the Lancashire League in their first season. He never played League football for Liverpool as he moved on straight after that season reached its conclusion.

X

X Files

Although there are few reports of ghoulish behaviour at Anfield, if an interesting tale is to be believed Liverpool were certainties to lift The Worthington Cup in March 2001 once Birmingham City got through to the final. All thanks to powers beyond this realm.

The story goes that when Birmingham obtained the land St Andrews was built on in 1906, it aggrieved gypsies who until that time had used it. A curse was said to have been put upon the club and that as a result they would never achieve major success. Attempts to lift the curse have been made including former manager Barry Fry urinating in each corner of the pitch.

However, 95 years on and despite a strong effort against The Reds City remain without a trophy to their name after losing the penalty shoot-out. It may be that fate was always going to smile on The Reds given the fact that Liverpool are one of the few clubs to have had a Romany on their books. Rabbi Howell played between 1897 and 1901 making 68 appearances. He is to date the only Romany ever to play for England earning a cap in 1899 against Scotland.

Liverpool have of course fallen victim to and benefited from unusual circumstances. Amongst the most memorable is the home game with Newcastle United in 1997 which had finished 4-3 to Liverpool as it had in the Anfield game between the two sides the previous season. Bookmakers offered odds of 100-1 on the event reoccurring. With little more than a quarter of the game remaining it seemed the bookies had got it exactly right. Liverpool were coasting to victory and lightening would not be striking twice. However, The Magpies pulled it back to 3-3 with minutes remaining courtesy of a bizarre goal by Warren Barton. 12 months earlier Liverpool were being held by the same score only for Stan Collymore to rifle home and secure the points in the dying minutes. Again there were seconds of the game left when Collymore's strike partner on that evening Robbie Fowler rose above everyone else to send a header home from six yards.

X-rays

Melwood currently has one of the most up to date medical units of any training ground in the country. This has more or less been so since the 1960s. However, plans to install an X-ray machine were dropped as it was thought to be an uneconomical measure as it would require specialist staff and the hospital facilities were already available on Merseyside.

Y

Ron Yeats

On signing Ron Yeats Bill Shankly described his new centre half as a colossus. As if to prove his point he invited journalists covering the story to come and take a walk around him. Considering he stood 6'2" tall and weighed approximately 14 stone Shanks' description was a fair one but he was a giant in much more than stature. He provided the cornerstone of a defence which would play a large part in not only Liverpool's assault on the First Division but in The Reds' battle for supremacy in Europe.

A £30,000 fee for the former slaughterhouse man was a major amount of money in July 1961 but these days Big Ronnie would fetch many millions of pounds on the transfer market.

He was appointed club captain almost as soon as the ink on his contract was dry. It was a role which he kept for nine seasons during which time he lead Liverpool to the Second Division Championship, two League Championships and a first ever FA Cup win. To date he is Liverpool's longest-serving post-war captain.

First team opportunities dried up at the turn of the 1970's. A new breed of young defenders were chomping at the bit and when the opportunity came their way they proved more than equal to it. After a decade at Anfield and over 450 appearances he made the short journey across the Mersey to take up a player/manager role at Prenton Park. After leaving Tranmere he remained out of the game until appointed as Anfield's Chief Scout in 1986. He still holds a post in the talent spotting department at Anfield.

You'll Never Walk Alone

When lifelong Liverpool fan Gerry Marsden covered a track originally written by Rogers and Hammerstein for the musical Carousel he had no idea that it would become the anthem of his beloved Reds. As every soccer fan knows that song was You'll Never Walk Alone.

It earned Gerry and the Pacemakers a hit in the 1960's at which time Anfield's resident DJ Stewart Bateman played it at each home game. The Kop's habit of singing current pop tunes as well as the traditional chants in support of their team made the record very popular on the terraces. When it began its descent from the charts it was replaced by another contemporary tune. That was the first and only week it hasn't been heard at the ground. Its absence caused such a stir that it was restored to the turntable for the next home game and every one since just before the teams run on to the pitch.

PFA Young Player of the Year Award

Securing the vote as the league's best young player is an honour usually given to a young man who has proved himself continuously over the course of a season against professionals with far more experience. Liverpool players have taken the award on four occasions. Three times it has been claimed by a striker which proves the quality club managers have been fortunate enough to select from. Ian Rush was the first winner in 1983.

Robbie Fowler was the next Liverpool recipient of the honour 12 years later. The goal scoring feats achieved by Michael Owen in 1998 secured him the accolade in his first full season.

One of the next young stars off the Liverpool production line Steven Gerrard enjoyed such a dominant season throughout 2000-01 that he was touted as a possible candidate for the senior award, but the 20 year old was a clear winner on the basis of his ability to pass, tackle and score more than his fair share of goals.

Youngest Player

Phil Charnock became the youngest Liverpool player to have taken part in a European game when replaced Steve Harkness in the 55th minute of the European Cup Winners' Cup game with Apollon Limassol on 16th September 1992. He was 17 years and seven months old at the time. He beat the previous mark set by Jamie Redknapp who was eight months his senior when he took part in the 1st leg of the 2nd round tie UEFA Cup game with Auxerre on 23rd October 1991.

Although both these players were younger than all that had gone before them the youngest player to sign for Liverpool and probably any other Football League club was Ray Lambert who joined The Reds as a 13 year old amateur in January 1936. He signed professional terms just before the outbreak of war in the summer of 1939 and may well have exceeded the records subsequently set had he not had to wait a full seven years to make an official appearance in the first team.

Tommy Younger

Tommy Younger played for Liverpool for three Second Division seasons in the

1950s. His signing proved a major coup as he was already a firmly established Scottish international and The Reds were still struggling to achieve promotion. The goalkeeper's position at Anfield had proved a huge void to fill since Cyril Sidlow left in 1951. He missed just six league games during his stay on Merseyside. Younger made a massive difference to the side and marshalled his defence like no keeper had for some time yet the top flight still eluded the club. A unique event took place in the 1957-58 campaign when Younger had to play up field for a large chunk of a game at Derby's Baseball Ground. He picked up an injury which affected his ability to keep goal. Substitutes were not allowed at the time so he moved into the outfield and actually played at centre-forward. He returned to Scotland in 1959 to become player-manager of Falkirk. Bert Slater came the other way to replace him in goal as part of the deal.

The FA Youth Cup

Despite having a vibrant youth policy Liverpool have only managed to claim the youngsters premier knockout competition on one occasion. In 1995-96 a young man called Michael Owen was instrumental in that victory and scored many vital goals to take The Reds through to the final.

Youth Policy

Apart from having the right profile and financial wherewithal to lure some of the best young talent to the club Liverpool have never lost sight of the fact that the best youth recruitment policy is to promote from within. Many Liverpool greats such as David Fairclough, Sammy Lee and Phil Thompson have all made the grade after joining the club's youth ranks. More recently Robbie Fowler, Michael Owen, Jamie Carragher, David Thompson and Stephen Gerrard have all made the first team. The grand total of their cost to the club - absolutely nothing.

An extension of this long held vision is the recently opened Liverpool Youth Academy in Kirkby, the first purpose built centre aimed at nurturing gifted youngsters in Britain. It boasts 12 floodlit pitches as well as indoor training facilities and a state of the art treatment centre. It is projected that around 200 youngsters will receive expert coaching and tuition at the centre.

Z

Zeal

One of the things each and every Liverpudlian demands from those lucky enough to wear the famous red shirt.

Christian Ziege

A controversial £5.5 million buy from Middlesbrough given that he had a get out clause in his contract allowing him to speak to another club if a bid of that amount was put in. He proved the subject of a protracted transfer during the summer of 2000. The incident left the Boro manager Bryan Robson livid and on returning to The Riverside Stadium Christian was roundly jeered by his old fans. The circumstances surrounding the move were held under investigation until after the season ended but led to Liverpool becoming the first Premiership team to be charged with making an illegal approach to a player.

The German can play on the left side of defence or midfield and showed an awful lot of potential during his first season in English Football. He also boasts one of the most awesome shots from the dead ball situation. Despite Gerrard Houllier expending so much money and effort securing his services the he was left on the sidelines for most of the campaign. A bout of injury combined with the form of Jamie Carragher in the left back position ensured he was given few chances. Exclusion from the side when fit led to a public exchange of views with the manager and a failure to figure even as a substitute in either the FA or UEFA Cup finals.

Before arriving on the North East he had started his career with Bayern Munich and AC Milan. A move back to his first professional club in exchange for left back Bixenete Liizarazu was touted during the spring of 2001 as were transfers to both Spurs and West Ham United. Talks were held with German champions Shalke 04 but the deal was abandoned after preliminary talks. Spurs finally secured his signature striking a £4 million deal with the Anfield board.

FC Zurich

The Swiss champions at the close of the 1975-76 season met Liverpool in the semi-final of the 1977 European Cup. Pundits ranked them as the weakest team left in the competition and in truth they were no match for Liverpool who booked their passage to the final in Rome courtesy of a 3-1 away win and a 3-0 win at Anfield. Phil Neal was on the mark twice in the initial encounter with Steve Heighway grabbing the other. In the return Jimmy Case scored twice. Kevin Keegan wrapped up the scoring late in the match.